W9-BJP-034

FEELING SECURE

IN A TROUBLED WORLD

CHARLES
STANLEY

OLIVER
NELSON ™

THOMAS NELSON PUBLISHERS
Nashville

Copyright © 2000 by Charles Stanley

All rights reserved. Written permission must be secured from the publisher to use or reproduce any part of this book, except for brief quotations in critical reviews or articles.

Published in Nashville, Tennessee, by Thomas Nelson, Inc.

Unless otherwise noted, Scripture quotations are from THE NEW KING JAMES VERSION. Copyright © 1979, 1980, 1982, Thomas Nelson, Inc., Publishers.

Scripture quotations noted KJV are from the KING JAMES VERSION.

Scripture quotations noted NIV are from the Holy Bible:
NEW INTERNATIONAL VERSION®. Copyright© 1973, 1978, 1984
by International Bible Society. Used by permission of Zondervan
Publishing House. All rights reserved.

ISBN 0-7852-7293-3

Printed in the United States of America
7 PHX 05 04 03

CONTENTS

GOD'S PROVISION IN TIMES OF DANGER AND TROUBLE

Everywhere we look in our world today, we see signs of very real trouble and danger. The troubles include natural disasters such as earthquakes, hurricanes, tornadoes, wild fires, and floods. They also include man-made dangers and turmoil, such as wars, crime, the creation of biological and chemical weapons, terrorist bombings, and conditions that lead to stock market meltdowns, rampant rioting, and coups intended to topple governments.

It seems at times that everything that *can* be shaken, is being shaken in our world, from the shaking of the natural earth to the shaking of the world's financial systems, from the shaking of time-honored institutions and traditions to the shaking of personal values and morals. We seem to live in an unsteady and insecure world.

All of us walk through countless metal detectors and have our movements monitored by security cameras, perhaps far more than we are aware. Most people live behind double-locked doors, many live behind security gates or have their possessions protected by security systems, and some even seek to arm themselves with personal weapons. Countless people are too afraid of violent attack to take a walk in their own neighborhoods after dark.

For many the terror is far more personal—fear that a spouse may come home drunk and become abusive either physically or verbally, fear that a former spouse or associate may turn to violent revenge, or fear of anger erupting from a total stranger in a public place. For some, the fear is rooted in suspicion, conjecture, and unconfirmed symptoms—fear of disease, fear that a spouse may not be faithful, fear that a child may be using drugs, or fear that a job may end tomorrow.

Is anything "sure" anymore? Can anything be counted on as being lasting, secure, and unchanging?

How is a Christian supposed to live in an insecure world?

How should a Christian react to threats of violence, acts of abuse, troubling news, or signs of imminent danger?

What is God's answer for our troubled world?

Those questions are at the heart of this Bible study.

Triumphant over Trials

There are three key biblical principles that I offer to you at the outset of this study. They are foundational principles that I hope you will remember as you study each lesson.

First, every person alive today is facing, has faced, or will face sorrow, trouble, difficulty, persecution, heartache, or a time of trial *at some point in his or her life.*

Even if you are not experiencing trouble at this very moment in your life, you very likely have experienced it in the fairly recent past, and with a great degree of certainty, I predict that you will experience trouble at some point in the future! None of us are immune to times of heartache, sorrow, grief, trouble, and unsettling change. Trouble is a fact of life.

Loved ones die.

Storms develop.

Markets rise and fall.

Relationships change.

And the evil in many hearts continues to reign in prideful rebellion against God.

We live in a fallen world.

Rather than see this as totally negative news, however, I encourage you to see a good side to this fact: You are not alone in your struggle with insecurity or trouble. Someone, somewhere, has experienced what you are experiencing. No matter what type of trouble seems to be overwhelming you, there is another person—usually far closer than you think—who knows from firsthand experience what you are going through and how you feel.

Yet another piece of good news is this: Men and women through the ages have experienced great persecutions, natural disasters, epidemics, plagues, wars, and trauma. Many of them were Christians and—by their overcoming lives, and by the words they have used to document their experiences—they give us shining examples of how to respond to trials with faith.

The book in the Bible we know as 1 Peter was written to a group of people who were facing a coming tidal wave of persecution and hardship. Much of what we will cover in this Bible study is based upon 1 Peter. Peter's words are like a beacon of light in a frightening world—both then and now.

Ultimately, the good news is that Christ Jesus knows your struggle with fear, doubt, and insecure feelings. He became fully human so that He might not only experience all you experience, but so that He might show us by example *how* to live triumphantly in difficult times.

Furthermore, Jesus Christ has sent the Holy Spirit to every person who believes in Him as Savior and who seeks to follow Him as Lord. The Holy Spirit is our great Comforter and

Counselor in times of trial. He is present with us *always*, fully bringing to bear in any situation the awesome and unlimited power and presence of almighty God.

You are *not* alone in your struggle. And you never will be alone in any struggle you ever face!

Second, regardless of the type of trial or trouble you experience, you have been given a wonderful gift from God to overcome it: *faith.*

Faith is not a nebulous entity that floats in and out of our lives in unknown quantities or in a mysterious way. Faith is an *ability* that has been imparted to every human being. No person is without faith, even though you may feel at times that your faith has vanished or that it is at a very low ebb.

Faith is an awesome power. It is the power that motivates us to act with confidence and boldness. It is the power that activates the work of the Holy Spirit in us, and through us. It is the power that brings about *change*. It is the force within us that gives us the ability to endure until God resolves our negative situation and turns it around so that His plans and purposes are enacted on this earth, our purpose in life is fulfilled, rewards are given to us for our eternal benefit, and His glory is revealed.

Each of us has been given the power to overcome fear. We have been given the power to bring about *change* in our personal lives and in our world.

Third, no trial or period of trouble lasts forever. At times, you may feel as if you have *always* experienced struggle or hardship. Some people seem to be hounded by troubles and trials all their lives. But the good news for every Christian is this: No problem we face on this earth lasts forever. All problems, trials, struggles, and troubles end the instant we enter into eternity.

In most cases, we also need to recognize that most troubles and trials we face on this earth do *not* last a lifetime. We often experience seasons of hardship or difficulty, instances of turmoil, and moments of crisis. These times of trouble may last an hour, a day, a week, a month, a year . . . even longer. But they do end.

If we will trust the Lord with an active faith to work in us and to teach us and to strengthen us in our time of trial, we have the assurance that we will emerge from our troubling experience stronger in faith, wiser in His ways, more confident in His power, and more like Jesus. Trials and troubles are often used by the Lord to chisel us, sand us, and mold us into greater conformity to the likeness of Christ Jesus' character.

A Rainbow After the Rain

God gave Noah a sign after the Great Flood—a rainbow appeared in the sky. With the rainbow came a promise from the Lord that He would never again completely destroy the earth by water. It was a promise that life would begin again, the generations would continue, and life had the potential for being better than it ever had been before.

The Lord holds out this same promise to each of us as we face troubled times. The Lord will walk with us *through* our trial all the way to the other side of it. His pledge to us is that our lives as Christians will *never end*. A new beginning is always possible for us—if not on this earth, certainly in our heavenly home. The work that we have done for the Lord *will* last and reap eternal benefit. Our life in the future will be vastly superior to our life in the past—in the form of both earthly blessings and eternal rewards.

Be encouraged today. We *can* feel secure even in the midst of a world that is being shaken to its foundation.

ONE

A Focus on Faith, Not Fear

There is a book that is a universal manual devoted to the development of a person's faith: the Bible. No other book has stood the test of time as the Bible has. No other book gives such a wealth of practical advice about how to apply one's faith. No other book couples practical advice about faith with so great an amount of inspirational motivation related to its actual *use*. No other book so completely details the rewards that come from an effective use of faith.

From beginning to end, this book you hold in your hands is intended for *Bible* study. I encourage you to refer to your Bible often as you read the lessons in it. Mark the passages, phrases, or words that hold special meaning to you. Write your insights in the margins of your Bible. In my opinion, a well-marked Bible is the genuine hallmark of a serious Bible student.

In a study about security in troubled times, it is easy to get sidetracked into discussions about the latest negative news, the most recent wave of trouble, or the most recent crime statistics. It is also easy to stray into discussions about self-preservation, hoarding resources, or new means of self-protection. Avoid those tendencies!

Stay focused on what the Bible has to say about your *faith*. As we discussed in the introduction, your faith—strong, alive, active, and effective—is your best resource for overcoming fear and for bringing God's positive solutions to bear on negative circumstances.

Keys to Study

You will be asked at various points in the lessons to identify with the material by answering one or more of these questions:

- What new insights have you gained?
- Have you ever had a similar experience?
- How do you feel about this?
- In what way do you feel challenged to act?

Insights

An insight is more than a new idea or fact. It is seeing a deeper meaning or the eternal truth of God's Word with greater clarity. It is almost as if you are encountering for the first time the full *impact* of God's Word to you on a particular matter.

You may have read the Bible many times, or have studied a verse or passage in depth. But then, God surprises you! Just when you thought you fully understood God's message, you discover a new level of meaning or gain a new dimension of understanding. You may find yourself saying, "Why didn't I see that before?" That moment of recognizing God's truth is a spiritual insight.

Insights are very personal. They often occur to us in relationship to a particular experience or situation in our lives. We suddenly have a knowing about what to do, what to say, how to act, or what to believe.

Insights are also associated with our *study* of God's Word. Every part of the Word of God is linked to every other part of the Word of God, and often these linkages are the points at which we gain spiritual insight. We find ourselves saying, "Why, this reinforces that. This clarifies that. This gives new depth or application to what I read in another part of God's Word."

Ask God to give you fresh insights every time you read your Bible. I believe He will answer that prayer.

When you have a spiritual insight, note it in your Bible. Your insight may be in the form of a question. Keep that question in mind as you continue to read God's Word. When you come to a conclusive answer, also note that in your Bible.

The more you look and listen for insights, the more you will experience them. Those who are intentional and focused in their search for personal application and new spiritual insights nearly always gain more from a Bible study than those who are reading the Bible in a more superficial, objective manner. And the more you note your insights, the greater your understanding will grow about the truths of God that run from cover to cover in the Bible.

Experiences

Each of us comes to God's Word with a unique set of personal experiences, difficulties, and accomplishments. Therefore, we each have a unique perspective as we read the Bible.

For example, a person who has been raised in church from childhood and is very familiar with Bible stories may have a different understanding of a passage from a person who is a new believer and is just starting to study the Bible. In a group, this difference in familiarity with the Bible can create problems, although this is not necessarily so.

As you begin your study, recognize that you are coming to the study with a unique background and that you can always learn something from others, even the most naive novice.

Regardless of differing degrees of Bible training, church attendance, or theological understanding, what we hold in common as human beings is *life*. All of us can point to times in our lives when the truth of the Bible encouraged us, confirmed something to us, convicted us, or comforted us in some way. We all have experiences about which we can say, "I know that truth in the Bible is real because of what happened to me."

Our experiences, of course, do not make the Bible true. The Bible is absolute truth, period. Nevertheless, as we share our experiences and how they relate to the Bible, we find that God's Word applies to the human experience in more ways than we have ever thought possible or personally experienced. We begin to see that the Bible speaks to each person, and it addresses each emotion and general situation that a man or woman may feel or encounter in life.

This is especially important as we explore ways in which to build our faith to overcome, endure, or confront times of trouble and trial. God's Word builds faith in many ways—and faith, in turn, is expressed in many ways in the Bible. Many methods for applying faith can be cited in the Scriptures, as well as numerous situations toward which faith may be directed. In sharing your faith experiences with others and hearing their experiences in return, allow your faith to be built up. God sometimes works in mysterious ways—mysterious to *us*, sovereignly wise and perfect from God's point of view—and no righteous method is beyond God's use.

Sharing experiences in your faith journey is important for your spiritual growth. Even if you are doing this study on your own, I encourage you to talk to others about your faith experiences and to be open to listening to others tell how the Bible has impacted their lives.

Emotional Response

Just as we have unique backgrounds, we have unique emotional responses to God's Word. No one set of emotions is more valid than another. You may feel great relief or take comfort in reading a particular passage; another person may find the same passage frightening or perplexing.

Face your emotions honestly. Your emotions are a gift of God to you in order to motivate you and allow you to express yourself in unique ways. Learn to share your emotions with others. Allow others to express their emotional responses without judgment.

As is true of experience, our emotional responses do not make the Bible true. And never are emotions to be the basis for faith. Your faith must always be based on what God says, not on what you feel. At the same time, you are wise to recognize that the Bible has an emotional impact on every person. You cannot read the Bible with an open heart and mind and not have an emotional response to it. At times you may be moved to tears, at other times you may feel great elation, longing, surprise, or hope.

Explore your own emotional responses. *Why* do you feel fear? *Why* do you respond the way you do? Especially in a study about security in troubled times, you may find yourself wanting to dismiss all fear or discomfort in your life. There are some situations in which fear is a very good response to have! There are some situations that *should* make us feel uncomfortable, cautious, or doubtful. We each can benefit greatly by identifying how we feel, and then digging a little deeper to uncover *why* we feel what we feel. This often is the starting point for our growing in faith and in courage.

In my experience with Bible study groups, I have found that it is far more valuable to share feelings than to share opinions. Scholarly commentaries have their place in teaching us the context and background of certain passages. Some people do have special insights into God's Word that are of benefit to everyone in a group setting. But, generally speaking, sharing opinions is not very productive in group study, and in some cases it can actually be counterproductive, leading to anger, mistrust, alienation, or frustration. When we share our feelings with one another, however, we become vulnerable with other people and we give them the freedom to be vulnerable with us in return. This vulnerability often can open us to hearing what is truly significant and faith-building in God's Word.

When we share our emotional responses, we grow closer to one another, and as a group, closer to the heart of God. A sense of community is built up.

Challenges

In reading God's Word we nearly always come to a point where we feel a deep stirring in our spirits, often a conviction that there is something we need to address or change in our attitudes, habits, or behavior. Sometimes this is a conviction of sin. At other times it is a clear call from God to engage in a new discipline or area of ministry.

God is never content with the status quo. He is always seeking our growth and our perfection in Christ Jesus. He prompts us to move forward in our Christian walk, and to move to ever-deepening levels of faith and devotion.

When we feel God challenging us, stretching us, calling us, molding and shaping us, our response must be, "Show me clearly what You desire for me to do." When He reveals to us a direction we are to take or a decision we are to make, we must be quick to obey.

Ultimately, God desires that we read His Word and then *do* what it says. The main goal of our Bible study is to apply God's Word in our daily lives and to become stronger witnesses of the love of God to every person we encounter. It is not enough for us simply to *feel* secure in troubled times. We must be quick to impart to others the confidence we have based on God's Word. It is not enough for us to clarify our insights, recall our experiences, or identify our emotions. We must live out the Christian life twenty-four hours a day, seven days a week, every week of the year—*regardless of the situations we may encounter in our troubled world, troubled neighborhood, or troubled home.* We are challenged to be doers of His Word and not hearers only (James 1:22).

Studying with Others

This book is designed for both individual and small group use. I strongly suggest, however, that you become involved in a small group Bible study on this topic, if at all possible. The value of a group study is that you will be confronted with insights, experiences, and emotional responses that are not your own—and that will serve to stretch and challenge you. You will also gain much from discovering that *every* person struggles with times of trouble, sorrow, pain, and hardship. You will discover new ways in which God shows His faithfulness to us as He walks with us through times of trial.

If you do not have someone to talk to about your insights, experiences, emotions, and challenges, I encourage you to take the lead in starting or hosting a small group study in your home. Perhaps you can talk to your pastor about organizing a Bible study group in your church. Not only will you grow in your understanding of God's Word, but you will be building relationships with fellow believers that can be invaluable—and especially so when crisis times arise.

Keep the Bible Central

Keep the Bible central to your study. Don't let a Bible study group turn into a support group or a therapy group. These types of groups have their time and place, but it is as we gather around God's Word—as if we are reading the manual that will make a life-or-death difference in our lives—that we truly grow in faith and become all that He created and designed us to be.

If you are doing a personal Bible study, you must be diligent in maintaining your focus on God's Word. Self-analysis is not the goal of this study. Growing up in the fullness of the stature of Christ is the goal.

If you are part of a group study, make certain that your conversations about God's Word don't stray into discussions of the latest "scare" stories, end-time prophecies, or signs of evil in the world. The goal of this study is to build faith, not fuel fear. Stay in the Word of God! (If you are interested in spiritual warfare or preparing for Christ's return, I encourage you to consider two Bible studies in this series that are directed at those topics: *Overcoming the Enemy* and *Preparing for Christ's Return*.)

Prayer

I encourage you to begin your Bible study sessions in prayer. Ask God to give you spiritual eyes to see what He wants you to see and spiritual ears to hear what He wants you to hear. Ask Him to give you new insights. Ask Him to recall to your memory those experiences that have the greatest bearing on what you are reading and that will be most beneficial for you to share with others. Ask Him to help you identify and clarify your emotional responses. Ask Him to reveal to you what He desires for you to be, say, and do.

As you conclude each study, ask the Lord to seal what you have learned in your heart so you will never forget it. Ask Him to transform you more into the likeness of Jesus Christ as you meditate on what you have learned. And above all, ask Him to reveal to you ways in which you can apply what you have studied and to give you the courage to live out His Word in your daily life.

At the outset of this study, I encourage you to consider these questions:

- *What do you hope to gain personally from this study? In what areas today do you feel a need for greater "security"?*
- *What is the foremost trouble, hardship, trial, or difficulty you are currently experiencing?*
- *How do you feel about Christ's ability and desire to protect you in our troubled world—spirit, mind, and body?*
- *Are you willing to confront your fears? Are you open to being challenged to confront more directly those situations around you that are problematic?*

TWO

THE
FOUNDATION FOR
OUR SECURITY

In 1 Peter, Peter is writing to a group of people who are facing a coming tidal wave of persecution and hardship under the Roman emperor Nero. A severe persecution of Christians in Rome had been instigated by Nero, and that wave of persecution was rapidly making its way eastward to the region of Asia Minor, which included Pontus, Galatia, Cappadocia, and Bithynia. Peter was writing to the churches that had been established in this region, the members of which were bracing themselves against a time of trial. Nobody knew how severe or widespread the persecution might be, or how long it might last.

Peter, of course, knew about suffering and difficult times. As an apostle of Jesus, he had watched Jesus be severely maligned and eventually tortured and crucified. He had witnessed the persecution of the early church by zealous Jews, first in Jerusalem and later in other cities throughout the area we know as Israel. He himself had been imprisoned on several occasions for the gospel's sake.

Peter's message is not one of dire warning or doom, however. His letter is filled with hope and the message of God's grace. His exhortation to the believers is that they must continue to *stand firm* in the faith. Peter writes to *encourage* the believers.

Peter gives the believers two main reasons they can and should feel "secure" even though hard times are on the horizon. In this lesson, we will explore these reasons, which are the cornerstone of any believer's security.

You Have Been Chosen by God

From the opening lines of his letter, Peter makes a bold statement that the Christians to whom he is writing have been *chosen* by God:

> Grace and peace be multiplied to you in the knowledge of God and of Jesus our Lord, as His divine power has given to us all things that pertain to life and godliness, through the knowledge of Him who called us by glory and virtue, by which have been given to us exceedingly great and precious promises, that through these you may be partakers of the divine nature, having escaped the corruption that is in the world . . . (2 Peter 1:2–4)

• *What new insights do you have into this passage of Scripture?*

_____

_____

Peter makes it very clear that God has given the believers four wonderful, awesome things:

- all things that pertain to life and godliness,
- a call to experience the Lord and to truly *know* Him,
- exceedingly great and precious promises that lead to their developing the very nature of Christ, and
- an "escape" from the corruption of the world.

As believers today, we have been given these same great gifts from God.

Gift #1: All things pertaining to life and godliness. The good news is this: Even though the world around us may be a teeming cauldron of sin, we do not need to partake of that sin. We can live free of it in our hearts and minds. Sinful human beings may hurt us, but they cannot force us to sin against God in our hearts. We can remain in right standing before the Father regardless of what any other person may say or do.

Furthermore, as believers in Christ, we have the sure hope of eternal life. Indeed, we are already living in that hope—no matter what happens to us, we will *never* be separated from our loving heavenly Father. Even though the world around us may be filled with death—we can choose to pursue life. Even if we ourselves face death, we can know with certainty that we *have* the gift of eternal life.

What the Word Says	What the Word Says to Me
[Jesus said,] "The thief does not come except to steal, and to kill, and to destroy. I have come that they may have life, and that they may have it more abundantly." (John 10:10)	----------------------------------
[Jesus said,] "For God so loved the world that He gave His only begotten Son, that whoever believes in Him should not perish but have everlasting life." (John 3:16)	----------------------------------
[Jesus said,] "I am the resurrection and the life. He who believes in Me, though he may	----------------------------------

die, he shall live. And whoever
lives and believes in Me shall
never die. Do you believe
this?" (John 11:25–26)

Gift #2: A call to experience the Lord and to truly know *Him.* No matter how difficult the circumstances around us may become, as long as we are alive, we have the opportunity to *grow* in our knowledge of the Lord Jesus Christ, to *grow* in our relationship with our loving heavenly Father, and to *grow* in our capacity to experience God's love and mercy.

Peter wrote of the "sufferings of Christ and the glories that would follow" (1 Peter 1:11). No matter what degree of pain and sorrow we may feel, Christ has felt that same pain and sorrow . . . *and far more.* Our ability to identify with Christ can grow through suffering if we will choose to see our suffering as an opportunity to know Him better.

When tragedies strike us, we can take one of two responses— to press in to God and seek to know Him better and rely on Him more fully, or to blame God and withdraw from Him. Peter calls the believers in Asia Minor to choose to draw ever closer to God when persecution comes.

• *In your life, how have you dealt with tragedy and pain? What has been your response to God in difficult times?*

What the Word Says

[The apostle Paul wrote,] "I also count all things loss for the excellence of the knowledge of Christ Jesus my Lord, for whom I have suffered the loss of all things, and count them as rubbish, that I may

What the Word Says to Me

----

gain Christ and be found in
Him . . . that I may know Him
and the power of His resurrection, and the fellowship of His
sufferings, being conformed to
His death, if, by any means,
I may attain to the resurrection
from the dead." (Phil. 3:8–11)

Our hope for you is steadfast,
because we know that as you are
partakers of the sufferings, so
also you will partake of the
consolation. (2 Cor. 1:7)

Gift #3: Exceedingly great and precious promises that lead to our developing the character of Christ. What is it that we learn as we go through hard times and press in to know God better? We learn greater and greater dependency upon God. We ultimately learn that there is no one else on whom we *can* depend totally and completely for the provision and protection we need. All other systems, and eventually all other people—even those who love us—will fail us because they are finite, limited human beings.

The more we learn to trust God, the more we learn that He is utterly trustworthy. He never fails us or forsakes us. He is present with us always to comfort us, guide us, and help us.

Jesus said of Himself that He only did what He first saw the Father doing (John 5:19). He was under the authority of the Father. He drew every aspect of His life, Being, character, and ability from the Father. His miracle-working and healing power was the Father's power. The mercy, love, and forgiveness He extended were the mercy, love, and forgiveness of the Father.

Jesus lived in the Father's presence, filled with the Father's own nature, even in a world that rejected Him, ridiculed Him, and eventually killed Him.

We are called to live in the same state of dependency upon the Father. No matter what any one does to us, no matter what may "happen" to us, we are to draw our identity and our character from the Father. We are to respond to negative situations as Christ Jesus would respond. We are to live in the joy and peace of our relationship with the Lord even when nothing around us seems joyous or at peace.

We are not called simply to *know* Christ, but to *learn* Christ—to become like Him and to manifest His character to the world around us.

What the Word Says	What the Word Says to Me
[Jesus said,] "The Son can do nothing of Himself, but what He sees the Father do; for whatever He does, the Son also does in like manner." (John 5:19)	-----------
[Jesus said,] "I can of Myself do nothing. As I hear, I judge; and My judgment is righteous, because I do not seek My own will but the will of the Father who sent Me." (John 5:30)	-----------
[Jesus said,] "I do nothing of Myself; but as My Father taught Me, I speak these things. And He who sent Me is with Me. The Father has not left Me alone, for I always do those things that please Him." (John 8:28–29)	-----------
For whom He foreknew, He also predestined to be	-----------

conformed to the image of His
Son, that He might be the
firstborn among many
brethren. (Rom. 8:29)

Gift #4: A genuine "escape" from the corruption of the world.
Peter and the other apostles knew that the real "persecutor"
of our lives is not a storm, a condition, a disease, or another
human being. The true persecutor of the believer is Satan. He
is the one who seeks to steal, kill, and destroy. He is the one
who seeks to ensnare us in sin to the point that we not only
suffer in sin, but die in sin.

The true escape for the believers in Asia Minor was not an
escape from Rome—it was the escape from Satan's snare that
they had *already* experienced. Our true escape today is not an
escape from a negative situation or circumstances, but an escape
from the eternally deadly nature of unforgiven sin.

Nothing can separate us from the love and mercy of God once
we have accepted Jesus Christ as our Savior. We are eternally
bound to Him. We are eternally "secure" in His forgiveness.
We are no longer in our sins and trespasses—the life that we
live is the eternal life of Christ Jesus.

What the Word Says

What the Word Says to Me

For though He was crucified in
weakness, yet He lives by the
power of God. For we also are
weak in Him, but we shall live
with Him by the power of
God. (2 Cor. 13:4)

I have been crucified with
Christ; it is no longer I who
live, but Christ lives in me; and
the life which I now live in the
flesh I live by faith in the Son of

God, who loved me and gave
Himself for me. (Gal. 2:20)

We have been united together
in the likeness of His death,
certainly we also shall be in
the likeness of His resurrection, knowing this, that our
old man was crucified with
Him, that the body of sin
might be done away with, that
we should no longer be slaves
of sin. For he who has died
has been freed from sin . . .
Reckon yourselves to be dead
indeed to sin, but alive to God
in Christ Jesus our Lord.
(Rom. 6:5–7, 11)

Ask yourself today: Will the God who has given me all things pertaining to life and godliness . . . the God who has called me to experience Christ and to know Him . . . the God who has given me great promises that I am in the process of being conformed to the character image of Christ Jesus . . . the God who has freed me from the bondage of sin and given me eternal life . . . will that God abandon me in a time of hardship?

Never!

God has a purpose for your life. He has elected you, chosen you, preselected you to live with Him forever. He is in the process of transforming you and conforming you into His own nature. He is perfecting you and making you whole—restoring you to the original design He had in mind for you from eternity past. You are *His child*. Even in the most dire of circumstances, you can live with a deep, inner assurance that God is *with you*, His Spirit resides within you.

• *How have you felt as you have read the verses above about God's great gifts to you?*

_____

_____

Sealed by the Holy Spirit

Paul's second great message of hope and encouragement to the believers in Asia Minor was this: You are guarded and made safe by the power of God.

The devil cannot penetrate the seal of the Holy Spirit on your life. The devil has no authority over your future. He cannot steal your divine inheritance or keep you from receiving God's promise of eternal life.

Paul wrote to the Romans:

> Who shall separate us from the love of Christ? Shall tribulation, or distress, or persecution, or famine, or nakedness, or peril, or sword? . . .
> Yet in all these things we are more than conquerors through Him who loved us. For I am persuaded that neither death nor life, nor angels nor principalities nor powers, nor things present nor things to come, nor height nor depth, nor any other created thing, shall be able to separate us from the love of God which is in Christ Jesus our Lord. (Rom. 8:35, 37–39)

• *What new insights do you have into this passage from Romans?*

_____

_____

The presence of God in the life of the believer is a certainty. God has not only called us and chosen us, but He now indwells us and He will never depart from us. The work that He has begun in us, He will finish . . . He will continue it until we are perfected and made whole according to *His* definition of perfection and wholeness. His presence with us abides forever.

What the Word Says	What the Word Says to Me
According to His mercy He saved us, through the washing of regeneration and renewing of the Holy Spirit, whom He poured out on us abundantly through Jesus Christ our Savior, that having been justified by His grace we should become heirs according to the hope of eternal life. (Titus 3:5-7)	
Now may the God of peace Himself sanctify you completely; and may your spirit, soul, and body be preserved blameless at the coming of our Lord Jesus Christ. He who calls you is faithful, who also will do it. (1 Thess. 5:23-24)	
In Him you also trusted, after you heard the word of truth, the gospel of your salvation; in whom also, having believed, you were sealed with the Holy Spirit of promise, who is the guarantee of our inheritance until the redemption of the purchased possession, to the praise of His glory. (Eph. 1:13-14)	

In summary, the two great messages of Peter are:
- God has chosen you as His beloved child and has given you the privilege of growing into the likeness of His Son, Jesus Christ, and of experiencing an intimate, eternal relationship with Him.
- God is with you, now and forever, to bring to pass all of the promises He has made to you in His Word.

Our security is based upon these two truths. God is with us—indeed, He dwells within us by the power of His Spirit—and He has a plan for us.

These truths form the bedrock of our security. They are solid footing for us when all of the sands seem to be shifting around us.

> •*What new insights do you have into God's provision for you so that you might feel secure in a troubled world?*

_____

_____

> • *In what ways are you feeling challenged in your spirit?*

_____

_____

THREE

A PROPER PERSPECTIVE IN A TIME OF TROUBLE

How are we to respond to troubled times? How are we to respond to distressing circumstances, grievous situations, or an inner "heaviness" that doesn't seem to lift?

First and foremost, we are to adopt a right perspective for viewing our problem. In 1 Peter we find five things to do when we face times of struggle, hardship, persecution, or pain. Each of these actions is related to our developing and maintaining a godly perspective.

Key #1: Reaffirm Our Position in Christ

As we studied in the last lesson, Peter established a foundation for the believers in Asia Minor who were facing impending persecution. He encouraged them that their security should always be based upon the fact that they were chosen, in Christ forever, and that they were always going to be in a position of being both guarded and guided by an omnipotent God.

The foremost thing you can do when facing trouble is to *reaffirm your position in Christ*. Make your position in Christ the perspective from which you view trouble.

As you face a time of trial, choose to "see yourself" as being saved, loved, and in relationship with an all-powerful, ever-present heavenly Father. As a believer, you are also part of the "body of Christ"—you are not alone.

Abigail, in stating her case before King David, said to him, "The life of my lord shall be bound in the bundle of the living with the LORD your God; and the lives of your enemies He shall sling out, as from the pocket of a sling" (1 Sam. 25:29). This is the same position in which we find ourselves—we are "bound in the bundle" of those whose souls have been redeemed by the Lord.

•*What new insights do you have into 1 Sam. 25:29?*

_____

_____

There are several facts we must believe and reaffirm as we "see" ourselves in Christ:

1. No problem or difficulty has the power to tear us from the grasp of Christ.
2. No problem or difficulty can do more harm than Christ can remedy.
3. No trial or time of trouble can destroy our salvation.
4. No pain or heartache is too great for Christ to heal.

• *Have you experienced these truths in your life? Cite specific examples.*

_____

_____

Key #2: Reaffirm That Your Trial Will Be Profitable

There is a vast difference between the person who views a trial or problem as if it is an unresolvable, devastating calamity and the person who views a trial or problem as being a difficulty from which he might learn, grow, or benefit. The person who sees a trial as 100 percent negative is going to be a person who benefits little from a trial and who is going to feel dejected, fearful, and frustrated for the duration of the trial.

In contrast, the person who sees a trial as having at least *some* benefit is going to be looking for that benefit . . . and finding it. He is going to feel more optimistic and hopeful and is likely to work harder to overcome the trial he is facing.

There are three questions we should ask in a time of trial:

1. What is the source of this trial or trouble? Some troubles are brought about by our own ignorance, negligence, carelessness, or willful rebellion. If trouble comes into our lives in one of these ways, the way *out* of the trouble is likely to be the opposite of what got us into the trouble! We may need more wisdom or information, we may need to be more diligent or careful, or we may need to repent of our rebellion and obey God's commandments.

If the trial or trouble is a natural disaster, we may need to reevaluate what we can do to prevent such a disaster in the future. None of us can "catastrophe-proof" our lives completely, but we can be wise about where we build, how we live, and what materials we use in our homes. We can build shelters from storms, and we can heed evacuation warnings.

If the trial or trouble is truly spiritual in nature, then spiritual warfare or spiritual deliverance may be the way "out" of the problem.

If the trial or trouble is in a relationship, improving the relationship—perhaps through mutual counseling—may be a solution.

Take a close look at the source of the trial. You'll likely find ways in which you can turn things around so you not only regain what you are in danger of losing or have lost, but so you also might improve your situation and prevent future trials.

• *In your life, have you had an experience in which identifying the source of your problem led to a solution and to preventive measures for the future?*

_____

_____

2. *What is the reason God has allowed this trial or trouble in my life?* God has allowed you to experience this struggle for a sovereign purpose. There is very likely something He desires to build, grow, change, or heal in your life, or in the life of someone close to you. Ask God to reveal to you His purpose.

Too many people *blame* God for their problems. God does not punish His children by sending them problems.

Others believe that all problems are from the enemy of their souls. They err in failing to recognize that God both *knew* about the problem long before it arose and God *could* have averted the problem if He had so desired. God may not create or instigate problems in our lives, but He does *allow* them. He uses problems to teach us valuable lessons. He allows problems so we might change our ways and become stronger, wiser, and more whole.

• *In your life, can you look back on a trial and see how God used it to teach you or change you?*

_____

_____

• *How do you usually respond or feel toward God when a problem arises?*

_____

_____

3. *What is the potential result or outcome of this situation?* Look for the best possible outcome. What is it you might learn? How is it you might grow through the experience? What benefits are possible?

Romans 8:28 tells us, "We know that all things work together for good to those who love God, to those who are the called according to His purpose."

Peter was quick to see a good reason for the trials that were coming to the believers:

> In this you greatly rejoice, though now for a little while, if need be, you have been grieved by various trials, that the genuineness of your faith, being much more precious than gold that perishes, although it is tested by fire, may be found to praise, honor, and glory at the revelation of Jesus Christ, whom having not seen you love. (1 Peter 1:6-8)

Peter regarded a trial as a time of *testing*—which he also likens to the "refining" process associated with fine metals. Gold and silver are put into blazing furnaces in order to liquefy them so that the dross, or the alloy metals, might rise to the top and be skimmed away, leaving the pure gold or silver behind. A trial can produce this same work in our lives. It can *refine* us and *purify* us so that we might bring greater praise, honor, and glory to Jesus Christ.

What the Word Says	What the Word Says to Me
He is like a refiner's fire And like launderers' soap. He will sit as a refiner and a purifier of silver . . . And purge them as gold and silver, That they may offer to the LORD An offering in righteousness. (Mal. 3:2–3)	_____
I will . . . refine them as silver is refined, And test them as gold is tested.	_____

They will call on My name,

And I will answer them.

I will say, "This is My people";

And each one will say, "The

LORD is my God."

(Zech. 13:9)

> • *Is there a difference in your feelings when you believe a problem has you "in the fire" and when you believe a problem has you "in a refiner's fire, purifying you into a more worthy vessel for bringing honor and glory to the Lord"?*

Key #3: See the Trial Against Eternity's Backdrop

A major shift occurs in our perspective when we take our eyes off our problem and put the focus on eternity. Against the backdrop of eternity, any trial we might experience on this earth is only momentary.

When we get our eyes onto the wonderful future we have with the Lord in heaven, any trouble or trial we experience here is going to seem like a "light affliction" (2 Cor. 4:17). What is a little trouble here in the light of an eternal future of glory and splendor with the Lord?

What the Word Says

Therefore we do not lose heart.

Even though our outward man is

perishing, yet the inward man is

being renewed day by day. For

our light affliction, which is but

for a moment, is working for us

a far more exceeding and eternal

What the Word Says to Me

weight of glory, while we do not look at the things which are seen, but at the things which are not seen. For the things which are seen are temporary, but the things which are not seen are eternal. (2 Cor. 4:16-18)

I heard a loud voice from heaven saying, "Behold, the tabernacle of God is with men, and He will dwell with them, and they shall be His people. God Himself will be with them and be their God. And God will wipe away every tear from their eyes; there shall be no more death, nor sorrow, nor crying. There shall be no more pain, for the former things have passed away."

Then He who sat on the throne said, "Behold, I make all things new." (Rev. 21:3-5)

Key #4: Look for Ways Your Faith Will Increase

As you face trials or troubles, focus on the ways in which you believe your faith is going to work and to grow.

First, anticipate that your faith *will* work. God has given you faith to use. He expects your faith to be effective in bringing about positive changes in your life, and in the lives of others around you.

Second, anticipate that your faith will become stronger as a result of the trouble you are experiencing. The more we use our faith, the stronger it becomes.

Third, anticipate that your faith will grow. The Bible describes three levels of faith:

- little faith—those who believe God can and hope He will
- great faith—those who believe God can and God will
- perfect faith—those who believe something is desired by God and, therefore, it is as good as done!

- *In your life, at what level of faith do you believe you function in most situations?*

_____

_____

The Lord gave a parable in which He taught that our faith is proven and it grows and increases *as we obey what the Lord tells us to do* (Luke 17:5-10). Great faith does not blossom overnight. It is the result of years of trusting and obeying the Lord—including trusting and obeying the Lord during difficult times, in the presence of difficult people, and at difficult tasks.

What the Word Says

The apostles said to the Lord, "Increase our faith."

So the Lord said, "If you have faith as a mustard seed, you can say to this mulberry tree, 'Be pulled up by the roots and be planted in the sea,' and it would obey you. And which of you, having a servant plowing or tending sheep, will say to him when he

What the Word Says to Me

----

has come in from the field,
'Come at once and sit down to
eat'? But will he not rather say
to him, 'Prepare something for
my supper, and gird yourself
and serve me till I have eaten
and drunk, and afterward you
will eat and drink'? Does he
thank that servant because he
did the things that were commanded him? I think not. So
likewise you. . ." (Luke 17:5–10)

[Jesus said,] "According to
your faith let it be to you."
(Matt. 9:29)

For in it [the gospel of Christ]
the righteousness of God is
revealed from faith to faith; as
it is written, "The just shall live
by faith." (Rom. 1:17)

Key #5: Look for Growth in Your Relationship with Christ

Just as you look for your faith to strengthen and to grow,
look for your relationship with Christ to deepen and become
more precious. Every trial or time of trouble is an opportunity
for you to trust Him more, love Him more, and find greater
joy and contentment in your relationship with Him.

As it has been said, "God uses 'where we are' to teach us
'who He is.'"

The more we see Christ Jesus *in the midst of our trials and
struggles*, the more we find reason for genuine praise. We do
not praise God *for* our situation, but *in* our situation. We do

praise God *for* the pain we feel, but for *who He is* as our Healer, Protector, Provider, Counselor, Comforter, and Friend. No matter how dark the day, it will seem brighter as we say, "Praise be to God! He is worthy to be praised!"

What the Word Says	What the Word Says to Me
Rejoice always, pray without ceasing, in everything give thanks; for this is the will of God in Christ Jesus for you. (1 Thess. 5:16–18)	
The LORD is righteous in all His ways, Gracious in all His works. The LORD is near to all who call upon Him, To all who call upon Him in truth. He will fulfill the desire of those who fear Him; He also will hear their cry and save them. The LORD preserves all who love Him, But all the wicked He will destroy. My mouth shall speak the praise of the LORD, And all flesh shall bless His holy name Forever and ever. (Ps. 145:17–21)	

Start with Your Perspective

Consider the two perspectives compared below:

<u>**Perspective #1**</u>	<u>**Perspective #2**</u>
• confusion about whether one has a relationship with God	• certain that one is bound together "in Christ" and is part of Christ's Body forever
• doubtful that anything good can come from the present difficulty	• optimistic that God can bring something good from the present trouble or difficulty
• blames God and others for the problem and has no hope for the problem to be resolved unless others change or circumstances change	• looks for the source, reason, and result of the problem so that the problem can be addressed and resolved quickly
• sees problem as monumental and lasting "forever"	• sees problem as momentary in the light of eternity
• regards a problem as contrary to faith or damaging to one's faith	• regards a problem as having the potential to strengthen and increase one's faith

Which perspective is more beneficial and productive for the person facing a time of trouble?

Before you can ever truly *feel* secure in a time of trouble, you must have the right perspective.

> • *What new insights do you have into the link between perspective and feelings of being secure?*

_____

_____

> • *In what ways are you feeling challenged in your spirit?*

_____

FOUR

THE UNSHAKABLE SECURITY OF OUR SALVATION

There are many Christians who believe that when tough times come their way, God is angry with them. They fear if God becomes angry enough, or is angry *often* enough, He may withdraw their salvation. Part of the insecurity they feel in a time of trial is an insecurity related to their relationship with the Lord.

Do you ever wonder if you are experiencing a difficult trial because you have lost your salvation?

Do you ever fear that you might be in danger of losing your salvation because of a tragedy, crisis, or time of trauma you are experiencing?

If so—this lesson is especially for you!

What Does It Mean to Be Saved?

For many people, confusion about their salvation results from a lack of understanding about what it really *means* to be saved. Salvation is not ours because we have:

- stopped a bad behavior in order to "get right with God;"
- joined a church,
- kneeled at an altar to say we are sorry for our sins; and
- added Christian disciplines such as prayer and
  Bible reading to our daily routines.

All of these things are "works" of some kind. Salvation comes from *faith*. It is the result of believing, not a by-product of doing.

Nicodemus, a very religious man in the time of Jesus, was shocked when Jesus told him that his good works as a Law-keeping Jew were inadequate for him to be born again spiritually. Jesus said to him:

> Most assuredly, I say to you, unless one is born of water and the Spirit, he cannot enter the kingdom of God. That which is born of the flesh is flesh, and that which is born of the Spirit is spirit. Do not marvel that I said to you, "You must be born again." The wind blows where it wishes, and you hear the sound of it, but cannot tell where it comes from and where it goes. So is everyone who is born of the Spirit . . .
>
> As Moses lifted up the serpent in the wilderness, even so must the Son of Man be lifted up, that whoever believes in Him should not perish but have eternal life. For God so loved the world that He gave His only begotten Son, that whoever believes in Him should not perish but have everlasting life. For God did not send His Son into the world to condemn the world, but that the world through Him might be saved.
>
> He who believes in Him is not condemned; but he who does not believe is condemned already, because he has not believed in the name of the only begotten Son of God. (John 3:5–8, 14–18)

• *What does it mean to you to be "saved"?*

_____

_____

•*What new insights do you have into this passage of Scripture from the Gospel of John?*

_____

_____

An act of believing and receiving. Jesus told Nicodemus that the "receiving" of God's provision for man's sin nature was a simple matter of believing. He referred to an Old Testament story in which the Israelites were experiencing a plague of poisonous snakes in their camp. All the Lord required of them was that they "look" upon the form of a bronze serpent lifted up on a pole, and they would live (see Num. 21:5–9).

Jesus said this same pattern would hold true for those who "looked" upon His death on the cross. All a person needs to do today in order to be saved from the consequences of their sin nature is to look at Jesus on the cross, believing that Jesus was and is forever God's sole provision for man's sin problem. A belief in Jesus as God's Son and as God's sacrifice for the sins of man is what saves a person. *Nothing less will do, but nothing more is required!*

What the Word Says

For by grace you have been saved through faith, and that not of yourselves; it is the gift of God, not of works, lest anyone should boast. (Eph. 2:8–9)

If we confess our sins, He is faithful and just to forgive us our sins and to cleanse us from all unrighteousness. (1 John 1:9)

If you confess with your mouth the Lord Jesus and believe in your heart that God has raised

What the Word Says to Me

....

....

....

....

....

....

....

....

....

....

....

Him from the dead, you will
be saved. For with the heart
one believes unto righteousness, and with the mouth
confession is made unto salvation . . . For "whoever calls on
the name of the LORD shall be
saved." (Rom. 10:9–10, 13)

A man is not justified by the
works of the law but by faith in
Jesus Christ, even we have
believed in Christ Jesus, that
we might be justified by faith
in Christ and not by the works
of the law; for by the works of
the law no flesh shall be justified. (Gal. 2:16)

A free gift to all who receive *it.* Salvation is a free gift of God
to those who will receive it. Salvation is not bestowed upon all
mankind, however, whether they want it or not. We must *choose*
by an act of faith to believe in Jesus and to receive Him as our
Savior.

> • *In your life, have you had the experience of believing in and
> receiving Jesus Christ as your Savior? If not, I encourage you
> to take that step of believing and receiving today!*

What Is It We Are Saved From?

When we accept Jesus Christ as our Savior, we are not "saved"
from difficulty, trial, or hardship in life. We are not "saved" from

being tempted or from ever having an encounter with an evil person. When we receive Jesus Christ as our Savior, we are "saved" from the eternal consequences that are associated with a person's *sin nature*. Salvation is a matter of the heart of man—it is not a matter of outer circumstances or external situations.

Every person has a choice to make. The Bible makes it very clear that there are those who are saved and destined for eternal life with God, and those who are not saved and are destined for a life apart from God. Jesus spoke very clearly about this in Matthew 25:

- "Cast the unprofitable servant into the outer darkness. There will be weeping and gnashing of teeth" (v. 30).
- "He will also say to those on the left hand, 'Depart from Me, you cursed, into the everlasting fire prepared for the devil and his angels'" (v. 41).
- "These will go away into everlasting punishment, but the righteous into eternal life" (v. 46).

Those who choose to believe in Christ Jesus are those who are saved. We each must do our own believing. Nobody else can believe on our behalf.

Sin is man's original nature. Sin against God is going beyond the boundaries established by God. It is not only a behavioral problem, however—one rooted in attitudes, motives, actions, and patterns of conduct. Sin is a "nature" problem, an identity or "state of being" problem. Man's sin nature is one of pride, greed, and total self-centeredness and self-will. Every person is born with this sin nature. Behavior is learned; our natural tendency to sin is not. A sin nature is inherent, and it is inherent regardless of the spiritual condition of our parents. It is part of our inheritance as fallen human beings, the descendants of Adam and Eve.

Now, a person might change his or her behavior by an act of the will. But a person cannot change his basic sin nature, regardless of how much "willpower" is exerted. We are incapable of transforming our spirits or of altering the core of our spiritual being. We are born with a "sin condition" that only God can correct.

The good news is that while we were in this helpless, ungodly state of unforgiven sin, God sent His Son, Jesus, to die for us so that we do not have to experience the consequence of our sin nature—which is separation and alienation from God. We *can* be transformed and made new in spirit through believing in Him.

What the Word Says

And you He made alive, who were dead in trespasses and sins, in which you once walked according to the course of this world, according to the prince of the power of the air, the spirit who now works in the sons of disobedience, among whom also we all once conducted ourselves in the lusts of our flesh, fulfilling the desires of the flesh and of the mind, and were by nature children of wrath, just as the others. (Eph. 2:1–3)

For when we were still without strength, in due time Christ died for the ungodly . . . God demonstrates His own love toward us, in that while we were still sinners, Christ died for us . . . For if when we were enemies we were reconciled to

What the Word Says to Me

God through the death of His
Son, much more, having been
reconciled, we shall be saved by
His life. (Rom. 5:6, 8, 10)

What Happens When We Accept Christ?

Two things happen simultaneously to a person who believes
in and receives Jesus as their Savior:

1. *Those who believe in Jesus and accept Him as their Savior
receive an everlasting quantity of life.* Jesus said to Nicodemus:
"Whoever believes . . . should not perish but have everlasting
life" (John 3:16). In many versions of the Bible the word *should*
is translated "will" or "shall." Whoever believes will *undeniably*
be given everlasting life by God. Jesus also said:

> Let not your heart be troubled; you believe in God,
> believe also in Me. In My Father's house are many man-
> sions; if it were not so, I would have told you. I go to
> prepare a place for you. And if I go and prepare a place
> for you, I will come again and receive you to Myself;
> that where I am, there you may be also. And where I go
> you know, and the way you know. (John 14:1–4)

• *How do you feel as you read this passage from John 14?*

_____

_____

2. *Those who believe in Jesus and accept Him as their Savior
receive a new quality of life.* Jesus also said to Nicodemus: "That
which is born of the Spirit is spirit" (John 3:6). The Holy Spirit
is sent to you by Jesus Christ the very instant you believe in
Christ and receive Him. It is the Spirit who causes your spirit
to be "reborn" or "made new."

There are two very important things you need to know
about this rebirth by the Spirit:

The Spirit does the birthing. You cannot will for it to be done.

Your part is to believe and receive. When we believe, the Holy Spirit enters into us and causes our old sin nature to be transformed into a new nature that is in the likeness of God. The transformation of our spirit is a sovereign work of God.

Part of believing is "confessing" your sins, which means to acknowledge or admit your sins. Confessing is owning up to your own sin nature and saying to the Lord, "I am a sinner. I have a sin nature. I ask You to forgive my sin nature and give me a new nature, with a heart to serve You. I believe in Jesus as the Savior and I receive Him into my life." When we believe in and receive Christ, God immediately acts to transform our spiritual nature.

Once a person has received the Holy Spirit into his or her life, that person will have a desire to love God, serve God, and walk in the ways of God. The person who is truly born anew spiritually will *want* to live according to God's commandments and to follow the daily leading of the Holy Spirit. The giving of the Holy Spirit is to help us walk in this new way of life.

We often hear the word *repentance* in association with salvation. To repent is to have a change of mind. The Holy Spirit dwelling within a person will cause a person to *want* to have a change of mind, and therefore, a subsequent change of behavior. Repentance comes in the wake of our salvation; it is the outgrowth of our receiving Christ.

Repentance and change come not only as the Holy Spirit prompts them, but also as the Holy Spirit helps a person to make changes! It is the Holy Spirit who is our enabler—He functions within us as the Spirit of Truth and the giver of courage and power. It is His *power* that links to our *will* to give us the only source of genuine *willpower* we can ever really have.

Nothing can alter God's definitive work in us. It is vitally important for you to understand that you cannot save yourself . . . it is equally important for you to understand that you cannot "unsave" yourself. Once a baby is born and is delivered from its mother's body, that baby can never go back into the womb. The same is true for us spiritually.

Once the Holy Spirit has birthed us into the family of God—delivering us from sin's bondage and giving us a brand-new nature—nothing that we do can ever cause the Spirit to "unbirth" us. The same holds true for any other influence, person, circumstance, or time of trouble. *Nothing* can impact our salvation once we are born anew spiritually. Our salvation is a certainty with God.

Furthermore, nothing can keep the Holy Spirit from continuing His transforming work in our lives. The Holy Spirit will continue to work within us until the moment we die. Now, we may reject His work. We may turn our backs on His convicting voice in our spirit. We may ignore His warnings. We may choose to go our own way. But we cannot separate ourselves from His efforts to mold us and conform us to the character-likeness of Christ Jesus.

> • *In your life, can you cite an experience in which you did not listen to the convicting voice of the Holy Spirit? What was the result?*

_____

_____

The Holy Spirit's Convicting Presence. Prior to our salvation, the Holy Spirit presents Christ to us and convicts us of our need to receive Him. We can so turn a deaf ear to His message that we no longer hear it. That does not mean, however, that the Spirit ceases to speak. We simply have become so hardened in our unbelief that we refuse to hear.

After we are saved, the Holy Spirit convicts us to repent and make changes in our lives so that we might experience greater wholeness and greater blessings from God. We can turn a deaf ear to His message, but He never quits speaking to us. The result will be that we are miserable and frustrated. The result will also be that we may enter into eternity without very many rewards awaiting us. But are we unsaved? Have we lost our salvation? No.

When we feel conviction in our spirits as people who have received Jesus as our Savior, that is the work of the Holy Spirit calling us to greater conformity to Christ. It is not a conviction that we are unsaved.

What the Word Says

Therefore, if anyone is in Christ, he is a new creation; old things have passed away; behold, all things have become new. (2 Cor. 5:17)

I have been crucified with Christ; it is no longer I who live, but Christ lives in me; and the life which I now live in the flesh I live by faith in the Son of God, who loved me and gave Himself for me. (Gal. 2:20)

You are not in the flesh but in the Spirit, if indeed the Spirit of God dwells in you. Now if anyone does not have the Spirit of Christ, he is not His. And if Christ is in you, the body is dead because of sin, but the Spirit is life because of righteousness. But if the Spirit of Him who raised Jesus from the dead dwells in you, He who raised Christ from the dead will also give life to your mortal bodies through His Spirit who dwells in you. (Rom. 8:9–11)

What the Word Says to Me

• *How did you feel as you read and meditated upon these verses of Scripture?*

_____

_____

Your Salvation and Times of Trial

Here is the point at which many Christians err: They know that their faith is linked to their salvation. When a time of trial hits them, they find their faith shaken. They experience moments of doubt and fear. And they wrongly conclude that their *lack* of faith is related to their *loss* of salvation.

That is *not* what the Bible teaches. Your faith gave entrance to the Holy Spirit into your life. Your believing in Jesus allowed the Holy Spirit to transform your sin nature into a new nature. But your faith did not *cause* you to be saved. The saving work in you was done exclusively and solely by the Holy Spirit.

The faith of the believer is infused with the faith of the Holy Spirit so that the believer can overcome evil, live a righteous life before God, understand God's Word as never before, and bring healing and deliverance to others in the name of Jesus Christ. A lack of faith can limit the effectiveness of a believer, but it cannot cause the Holy Spirit to leave that person's spirit.

When a time of trial hits, the proper response for the born-again believer in Christ Jesus is this:

• God knows all about this situation and He knows all about me personally. He knows fully how this situation impacts me, and He knows what He has planned and purposed for my life.
• God loves me, has forgiven me from my sins, and by the power of His Holy Spirit, dwells within me. He is at work in me to perfect me, make me whole, and conform me to the character-likeness of Christ Jesus. He will not give up on His work in me.

• No matter what happens to me, I can be completely secure in my spirit, knowing that I am in Christ and Christ is in me. I have an eternal home and a lasting, eternal, unshakable relationship with almighty God—my loving heavenly Father.

• Nothing about the trial, trouble, heartache, grief, sorrow, or pain I am currently experiencing in any way can change or alter the fact of my salvation.

Feeling secure in *spirit* is the best feeling of security a person can ever have. And especially so when nothing else in a person's life seems certain.

•*What new insights do you have into the importance of feeling secure in your spirit?*

_____

_____

• *In what ways are you feeling challenged today?*

_____

_____

(If you would like to explore the topic of eternal security further, I encourage you to get the book in this study series entitled *Understanding Eternal Security—Experiencing the Assurance of Your Heavenly Father's Unconditional Love.*)

FIVE

A READINESS FOR ROUGH TIMES

In many instances, rough times blindside us. They seem to come "out of the blue."

In other cases, however, we *know* that we are facing a rough time ahead, or we *know* that in all likelihood a tough time is inevitable. For example, parents might anticipate an "empty nest" as their teenagers mature and prepare to leave home; a family might anticipate grief as an elderly parent ages; a family might anticipate the rough time of moving and adjusting to a new city as the possibility of a promotion and relocation appears on the horizon; a person might anticipate the *possibility* of a storm or natural catastrophe if he chooses to live in an area prone to earthquakes, tornadoes, river flooding, forest fires, or hurricanes.

There is much that we can do to prepare for rough times, both in the natural and in the emotional realms of life. In this lesson, we will focus on five things that Peter suggests we do to prepare ourselves spiritually for a potential time of trouble or persecution.

1. Gird Your Minds for Godly Action

In Bible times, both men and women wore long outer garments. These could become a hindrance to a person who might be running or walking swiftly, walking through streams, or working at certain tasks. At times, a person found it better to "gird up" a garment by tucking a portion of it into the "girdle" at the waist. To "gird up" literally means to secure with a girdle or a wide belt.

What does this mean to us in the spiritual realm? It means that we are to remove from our lives those things that are a hindrance to us. We are to have the right *attitude*—removing from our lives anger, hostility, fear, doubt, worry, resentment, or any other negative feeling that can keep us from focusing positively on getting through the rough time and emerging stronger and more whole in its aftermath.

Peter wrote:

> Therefore gird up the loins of your mind, be sober, and rest your hope fully upon the grace that is to be brought to you at the revelation of Jesus Christ; as obedient children, not conforming yourselves to the former lusts, as in your ignorance; but as He who called you is holy, you also be holy in all your conduct. (1 Peter 1:13–15)

A person who enters a rough time focused on himself, simply living from day to day and following the whim of the moment, is going to be a person who feels doubly "hit" when a difficult time emerges: He will be unprepared emotionally for both the *possibility* and the *reality* of such a trial.

Peter called the believers to get serious about their lives and their future, to seek to conform themselves to the holy character of Jesus Christ, and to remain hopeful. These are all attitudes that the believer can *choose* to adopt.

> • *Recall an experience in your life in which you had time to prepare yourself emotionally for a difficult time. Recall an experience in your life for which you felt totally unprepared emotionally and spiritually. Cite the differences between the two experiences.*

• *How do you feel when you know you have prepared yourself as well as possible for an impending difficulty?*

_____

_____

2. Keep Sober in Your Spirit

What does it mean to be "sober" in spirit? Does it mean that Christians should be long-faced, sorrowful creatures without any expression of joy or happiness? No! In fact, Jesus spoke very clearly that Christians *at no time* should reflect a lack of joy or hope in order to appear more pious (see Matt. 6:16–18). Even in troubled times, we are to remain hopeful and confident in our faith.

To be sober means to

• have balanced judgment,
• exhibit a lack of panic,
• be steady and watchful,
• remain balanced.

The sober person does not grab on to a quick-fix promise or heresy, but rather, remains measured and deliberate in his believing and behaving. The sober person *responds* to life, rather than reacts to it.

What the Word Says	What the Word Says to Me
[Jesus taught,] "When you fast, do not be like the hypocrites, with a sad countenance. For they disfigure their faces that they may appear to men to be fasting. Assuredly, I say to you, they have their reward. But you, when you fast, anoint your head and wash your face,	

so that you do not appear to men to be fasting, but to your Father who is in the secret place; and your Father who sees in secret will reward you openly." (Matt. 6:16–18)

You are all sons of light and sons of the day. We are not of the night nor of darkness. Therefore let us not sleep, as others do, but let us watch and be sober. For those who sleep, sleep at night, and those who get drunk are drunk at night. But let us who are of the day be sober, putting on the breast- plate of faith and love, and as a helmet the hope of salvation. For God did not appoint us to wrath, but to obtain salvation through our Lord Jesus Christ, who died for us, that whether we wake or sleep, we should live together with Him. (1 Thess. 5:5–10)

Be serious and watchful in your prayers. (1 Peter 4:7)

Denying ungodliness and worldly lusts, we should live soberly, righteously, and godly in the present age, looking for the blessed hope and glorious

appearing of our great God and
Savior Jesus Christ.
(Titus 2:12–13)

• *Recall a crisis experience in your life when you reacted with panic. How did you feel? What was the result?*

• *Recall a crisis experience in your life when you responded in an intentional, deliberate way. How did you feel? What was the result?*

---

3. Fix Your Hope on God's Grace

Peter wrote, "Rest your hope fully upon the grace that is to be brought to you at the revelation of Jesus Christ" (1 Peter 1:13).

To rest your hope fully means to *set* your hope, to *fix* it, to *attach it firmly*. Hope does not exist in a vacuum. It is always directed toward something that still lies ahead. It is aimed *at* something. We hope we will be successful . . . we hope we will be invited . . . we hope we will win . . . we hope for a good result . . . we hope we will be the one who gets the job . . . we hope the weather will be nice for our vacation.

Peter tells the new believers to fix their hope firmly and fully on God's grace—which is the "loving work of God in our lives"—that is going to be revealed to them in the troubled time ahead.

The Lord allows us to experience rough times so that He might accomplish His purposes in us, and then through us, accomplish His purposes in the lives of others. Our *hope*, therefore, must be that the Lord's purposes will be fulfilled in us and in others.

As we prepare for a rough time, our spiritual attitude should be, "I have great hope about what the Lord is going to teach me and reveal to me during this time," or "I have hope that God is going to bring me through this so that I become stronger, wiser, and more faithful in my walk with Him."

- *Recall a difficult experience in your life that you entered with the hope that the Lord would bring you to a successful resolution or outcome. How did you feel? What were the results?*

_____

_____

- *Recall a difficult experience that you entered without hope. How did you feel? What were the results?*

_____

_____

What the Word Says

What the Word Says to Me

And now, Lord, what do I wait for? ....

My hope is in You. ....

Deliver me from all my ....

transgressions; ....

Do not make me the reproach ....

of the foolish. (Ps. 39:7–8) ....

For You are my hope, O Lord God; ....

You are my trust from my youth. ....

By You I have been upheld from ....

birth; ....

You are He who took me out ....

of my mother's womb. ....

My praise shall be continually ....

of You. (Ps. 71:5–6) ....

You are my hope in the day ....

of doom. (Jer. 17:17) ....

Be kindly affectionate to one ....

another with brotherly love . . . .

rejoicing in hope, patient in   ---
tribulation, continuing stead-   ---
fastly in prayer. (Rom. 12:10, 12)   ---

Now may the God of hope fill   ---
you with all joy and peace in   ---
believing, that you may abound   ---
in hope by the power of the   ---
Holy Spirit. (Rom. 15:13)   ---

4. Do Not Fall Back into Your Old Life

There are times when a Christian faces a rough time, and, in panic, he or she reverts to the old ways, habits, and patterns of thinking and responding. At other times, we see tough times ahead and we resort to the "world's systems"—we look to the way the world solves problems and avoids crises as a pattern for handling our own difficulties.

Peter admonished the believers: Avoid "conforming yourselves to the former lusts"—which was the way, he said, they had lived in their "ignorance" before accepting and knowing Christ.

As believers, we have been given the mind of Christ, and, therefore, we have been given a new way of thinking and responding to life's problems. The old ways of thinking and responding that are habitual to us must be *put off*. We must choose to think and act in different ways.

As you prepare yourself for a rough time, ask the Lord:

- How do *You* want me to face this problem and resolve it?
- How do *You* want me to prepare for this season that appears to be a difficult one?
- How do *You* want me to respond emotionally to this impending situation?
- What should I say or do in the coming situation or trial that will be pleasing to *You*?

Too often a person seeks to escape the brunt of rough times, or to escape the pain and hurt that he believes will be associated with a difficult period, by surrounding himself with a layer of "things." He hopes that a padding of luxury or material sufficiency will make the tough time easier to endure. Others turn to various substances and experiences that they hope will "numb" them to the coming pain or to the reality they fear will be unpleasant.

The Lord desires that we face our rough times with boldness and confidence, trusting in Him—and in Him alone—to give us the comfort and the courage we need. The Lord desires that we face rough times with all of our faculties fully functioning. We need to *choose* to stay physically and emotionally well and strong so that we can face fully, and effectively, the coming crisis.

- *In your life, can you cite some of the "old patterns"—habits or ways of thinking—that you have used in the past to deal with impending difficulties? Are these truly godly patterns?*

_____

_____

- *In what ways are you feeling challenged in your spirit to adopt a new way of responding to impending difficulty?*

_____

_____

What the Word Says

Put off, concerning your former conduct, the old man which grows corrupt according to the deceitful lusts, and be renewed in the spirit of your mind, and that you put on the new man which was created according to God, in true

What the Word Says to Me

_____

_____

_____

_____

_____

_____

_____

_____

righteousness and holiness. Therefore, putting away lying, "Let each one of you speak truth with his neighbor," for we are members of one another. "Be angry, and do not sin": do not let the sun go down on your wrath, nor give place to the devil. Let him who stole steal no longer, but rather let him labor, working with his hands what is good, that he may have something to give him who has need. Let no corrupt word proceed out of your mouth, but what is good for necessary edification, that it may impart grace to the hearers. And do not grieve the Holy Spirit of God, by whom you were sealed for the day of redemption. Let all bitterness, wrath, anger, clamor, and evil speaking be put away from you, with all malice. And be kind to one another, tender-hearted, forgiving one another, even as God in Christ forgave you. (Eph. 4:22–32)

5. Be Holy

What does it mean to be holy? Holiness is not an external demeanor—it definitely is not a "holier-than-thou" attitude or a pious set of behaviors intended to impress another person.

"Holy" in the Greek language is *hagias*. The word means "to be sanctified" or "to be cleansed and set apart" for God's purposes.

As a Christian, you do not belong to yourself. You now belong to God—you are His child, His servant, His beloved witness. You have a "separate" identity from that of the world at large—you have become part of the family of God; you are no longer just a general member of the "family of mankind."

To be "holy" means that we remain submissive to the Holy Spirit so that His holiness flows through us. Our righteousness is not something we can manufacture, think up, or develop on our own. Our righteousness is *His* righteousness manifested in us.

In facing tough times, it is vitally important that you set your heart and mind to *respond* to the situations you will encounter *as Jesus Christ would respond*. Choose to see yourself as being part of the body of Christ, a beloved child of almighty God, your heavenly Father. Choose to respond in a godly way, in spite of what others may do to you or say about you. Choose to pursue a path of righteousness—which is saying and doing the "right" things from God's perspective—regardless of how you may feel in any given moment or situation. We must choose to be holy, and to allow the holiness of the Spirit to operate in our lives. As Peter wrote, "He who called you is holy, you also be holy in all your conduct, because it is written, 'Be holy, for I am holy'" (1 Peter 1:15–16).

• *What insights do you have into what it means to be holy—to be "separate" from the world and "set apart" for God's purposes?*

_____

_____

What the Word Says	What the Word Says to Me
He chose us in Him before the foundation of the world, that we should be holy and without blame before Him in love. (Eph. 1:4)	....

Do not be conformed to this world, but be transformed by the renewing of your mind, that you may prove what is that good and acceptable and perfect will of God. (Rom. 12:2)

Therefore, as the elect of God, holy and beloved, put on tender mercies, kindness, humility, meekness, longsuffering; bearing with one another, and forgiving one another . . . But above all these things put on love, which is the bond of perfection. (Col. 3:12–14)

Do not love the world or the things in the world. If anyone loves the world, the love of the Father is not in him. For all that is in the world—the lust of the flesh, the lust of the eyes, and the pride of life—is not of the Father but is of the world. And the world is passing away, and the lust of it; but he who does the will of God abides forever. (1 John 2:15–17)

You are of God, little children, and have overcome them, because He who is in you is greater than he who is in the world . . . we know the spirit of truth and the spirit of error. (1 John 4:4, 6)

Ready for Trouble

As you have read and studied the five ways in which Peter exhorted the early believers to be ready for a coming wave of persecution, you may have thought to yourself, *This is the way a person should live* all *the time.* That's absolutely correct.

If we choose to do the things Peter said, we will live in a state of "spiritual readiness" for any problems that may come our way, expected or unexpected.

Gird your minds—remove from your life all attitudes that might hinder a rapid and effective response to trouble.

Keep sober in your spirit—watchful, balanced, and steady in your faith.

Fix your hope on the grace of God—which is, and will continue to be, manifested toward you.

Refuse to revert to old patterns, habits, and worldly ways of thinking and responding—choose to respond in a godly manner.

Invite the Holy Spirit to work in you and through you so that you might express the true nature of God, your heavenly Father, to others around you.

The person who lives in this manner is not only ready for rough times but ready for *all* times and seasons of life!

• *In what ways are you feeling challenged in your spirit today?*

_____

_____

SIX

THE BELIEVER'S CONDUCT IN A CRISIS

Once a crisis engulfs us, how are we to behave? What actions are we to take? What are we to do?

Peter makes this general but very powerful statement to the early church as it faced a time of persecution: "Conduct yourselves throughout the time of your stay here in fear" (1 Peter 1:17).

Peter was not referring to being scared or frightened of circumstances or evil people. The fear to which he was referring was a "holy awe of the Lord." We are to conduct ourselves with "fear of the Lord"—reverence, awe, and submission to His majesty. We are to be more in awe of God and His power than we are in awe of man's power or nature's power.

• *How does "fear of man" or "fear of nature" differ from a "holy, awesome fear of God" in the emotional realm? How do you feel and respond when you are afraid of someone?*

_____

_____

• How do you feel and respond when you are in awe of God's power and majesty?

_____

_____

A Holy Awe of God's Power to Judge

Those who truly fear God must always remember that God not only *can* but *will* punish the wicked and bring about His purposes and righteousness. We are to hold in high regard—truly to stand in awe of and to be ever mindful of—the fact that God is a God of absolutes and a God of perfect judgment.

There is a divine balance between God's love and God's judgment. On the one hand, God is merciful, loving, and forgiving to those who turn to Him and receive His forgiveness. He is long-suffering in His patience, allowing men and women numerous opportunities to turn to Him, confess their sins, and believe in Jesus Christ as their Savior.

But on the other hand, God is a judge who judges in righteousness according to the absolutes of His Word. God moves decisively against those who are rebellious against Him and against those who injure His people. God never winks at sin. All sin is subject to the consequences of suffering, sorrow, and death (Rom. 6:23).

Far more than we fear what man *might* do, we must fear what God *can and will do* regarding sin.

What the Word Says	What the Word Says to Me
For the wages of sin is death, but the gift of God is eternal life in Christ Jesus our Lord. (Rom. 6:23)	....
Do you not know that to whom you present yourselves slaves to obey, you are that	....

one's slaves whom you obey, whether of sin leading to death, or of obedience leading to righteousness? (Rom. 6:16)

[Jesus said,] "Do not fear those who kill the body but cannot kill the soul. But rather fear Him who is able to destroy both soul and body in hell." (Matt. 10:28)

•*Whom do you truly fear today? Are you more afraid of what people—or a specific person—might say or do against you, or what God will say and do?*

What Does It Mean to Live in "the Fear of the Lord"?

There are several practical manifestations of a life lived in "fear of the Lord" or "awe of the Lord" and these will be the focus of our study.

1. *The first manifestation of those who truly live in "fear of the Lord" is obedience to God's commandments.* The Lord has given us very specific commandments in His Word, and He expects us to keep those commandments *without regard to circumstances or situations.* No matter what others may say to us in offering us an alluring, positive, good-sounding "alternative plan" to God's commandments, we must never choose to follow their advice. It is a plan or scheme that is of man's design, not God's. God's Word is very clear. The problem most Christians have is *not* that they do not *understand* God's standards for right and wrong, but that they choose not to *obey* what God has said.

A crisis is never a justification for sin. No crisis should ever be used as an excuse to overlook or disobey God's commandments.

What the Word Says

In the multitude of dreams and
many words there is also vanity.
But fear God. (Eccl. 5:7)

Let us hear the conclusion
of the whole matter:
Fear God and keep His
commandments,
For this is man's all.
For God will bring every work
into judgement,
Including every secret thing,
Whether good or evil.
(Eccl. 12:13-14)

The statutes, the ordinances,
the law, and the commandment
which He wrote for you, you shall
be careful to observe forever; you
shall not fear other gods. And the
covenant that I have made with
you, you shall not forget, nor shall
you fear other gods. But the
LORD your God you shall fear;
and He will deliver you from
the hand of all your enemies.
(2 Kings 17:37-39)

*Read Leviticus 19:13-14; 19:32;
25:36; and 25:43.* Note that these
verses, which are related to very
specific commandments, all
include a phrase admonishing
obedience: "Fear your God."

What the Word Says to Me

2. *A second manifestation of those who truly live in "fear of the Lord" is a desire to be like Jesus.* Those who truly love Jesus as their Savior and Lord want to be *like* Jesus.

Jesus lived in complete obedience to His Father. He did only what the Father revealed to Him to do; He spoke only what the Father prompted Him to say. What Jesus did, we are to do—not to the "best of our ability," but to the best of the Holy Spirit's ability within us! The Holy Spirit empowers us to live as Jesus lived. It is our responsibility to ask the Holy Spirit to guide us, help us, counsel us, and to give us the ability to obey. The more we allow the Holy Spirit to work in us and through us, the more we are enabled to *be* like Jesus and to *do* what He did.

Jesus knew what it meant to face a crisis. If there was ever a crisis in a person's life, it was the Cross in the life of Jesus! Jesus knew *how* to face that crisis—in complete submission to the Father's will. Jesus knew both what to say and what to do in the final hours of His earthly life.

When you are in a crisis, ask yourself, What would Jesus say and do? Ask the Holy Spirit to show you how Jesus would respond and to help you respond as He would respond.

What the Word Says

[Jesus said,] "When the Helper comes, whom I shall send to you from the Father, the Spirit of truth who proceeds from the Father, He will testify of Me. And you also will bear witness." (John 15:26–27)

[Jesus said,] "When He, the Spirit of truth, has come, He will guide you into all truth; for He will not speak on His own authority, but whatever He hears He will speak; and

What the Word Says to Me

He will tell you things to come.
He will glorify Me, for He will
take of what is Mine and declare
it to you." (John 16:13–14)

[Jesus said,] "Now when they
bring you to the synagogues
and magistrates and authorities, do not worry about how
or what you should answer, or
what you should say. For the
Holy Spirit will teach you in
that very hour what you ought
to say." (Luke 12:11–12)

• *How did you feel as you read the verses above?*

3. *A third manifestation of those who truly live in "fear of the Lord" is courage.* Those who fear mankind and fear natural dis-aster experience a panic that paralyzes. Those who fear the Lord with a holy awe experience a courage that mobilizes them to act!

Throughout the Scriptures we find God's challenge to His people to live in confidence and to respond boldly and coura-geously to life.

Joseph of Arimathea. Joseph of Arimathea found himself in something of a crisis. Jesus had been crucified and His disci-ples had scattered and gone into hiding. But "Joseph of Arimathea, a prominent council member, who was himself wait-ing for the kingdom of God, coming and taking courage, went in to Pilate and asked for the body of Jesus" (Mark 15:43).

Peter and John. When the priests, temple leaders, and Sad-ducees "saw the boldness of Peter and John, and perceived that they were uneducated and untrained men, they marveled.

And they realized that they had been with Jesus" (Acts 4:13). These leaders threatened Peter and John never to speak or teach in the name of Jesus, but they answered, "We cannot but speak the things which we have seen and heard" (v. 20).

Were Peter and John intimidated by this encounter with the religious authorities in Jerusalem? No. They immediately returned to the believers and reported what had happened. And the believers prayed for them, "Now, Lord, look on their threats, and grant to Your servants that with all boldness they may speak Your word, by stretching out Your hand to heal, and that signs and wonders may be done through the name of Your holy Servant Jesus" (Acts 4:29–30).

Paul. After Paul had encountered Jesus in an experience on the road to Damascus, he "preached boldly at Damascus in the name of Jesus" even though many there distrusted him and counted him as an enemy. (See Acts 9:27.)

Paul and Barnabas. When envious Jews began to contradict and oppose Paul's ministry in Antioch in Pisidia, we read that "Paul and Barnabas grew bold and said, 'It was necessary that the word of God should be spoken to you first; but since you reject it, and judge yourselves unworthy of everlasting life, behold, we turn to the Gentiles'" (Acts 13:46).

Rather than cower in the face of crisis or conflict, the early believers became *bold*. They experienced a manifestation of courage in their lives that they knew with certainty was the work of the Holy Spirit in them.

When you are in a crisis, ask the Lord to give you boldness and courage to speak and do what the Lord prompts you to speak and do!

What the Word Says	**What the Word Says to Me**
The righteous are bold as a lion. (Prov. 28:1)	....
Even after we had suffered before and were spitefully	....

treated at Philippi, as you know,
we were bold in our God to
speak to you the gospel of God
in much conflict. (1 Thess. 2:2)

[Paul asked the believers at
Ephesus to pray for him:] That
utterance may be given to me,
that I may open my mouth
boldly to make known the
mystery of the gospel, for which
I am an ambassador in chains;
that in it I may speak boldly, as
I ought to speak. (Eph. 6:19–20)

He Himself has said, "I will
never leave you nor forsake
you." So we may boldly say:
"The LORD is my helper;
I will not fear.
What can man do to me?"
(Heb. 13:5–6)

Our Threefold Response in a Crisis

In summary, Paul advises a threefold response in a time of crisis:

    1. Keep God's commandments.

    2. Ask the Holy Spirit to help you do what Jesus would do.

    3. Have courage! Be bold in your witness to Christ and in your presenting the truth of God.

This should be our response to *all* of life, but especially in crises it is important for us to renew our obedience, our commitment to Christ, and our reliance upon the Holy Spirit.

Crises come into every person's life. They tend to arise unexpectedly and quickly. The more we make obedience to God's commandments a way of life . . . the more we rely every day upon the Holy Spirit . . . and the more we display courage in standing up for what is right on a daily basis, choosing to go against the tide in making godly decisions and taking godly actions . . . the more we will be ready for crises when they come.

> • *What new insights do you have into how to respond to crisis situations?*

> _____

> _____

> • *In what ways are you feeling challenged in your spirit?*

> _____

> _____

SEVEN

LIVING AS A VICTOR

(EVEN WHEN YOU SEEM TO BE LOSING THE BATTLE)

What would you most like to change about your circumstances today? Most people would like to change *something* in their lives: perhaps their job, a family situation, or the state of their health. Some would like to see changes in their finances, others might like to move to a new city.

Why do most people want to make changes? In a great percentage of the cases, the changes are ones that the person believes will make him happier, more at peace, or more secure.

The Bible challenges us *not* to seek happiness, peace, and security through external changes in our lives, but rather through internal ones. A Christian is empowered to live "above circumstances," not "under the circumstances," as we commonly say.

The apostle Paul was living under house arrest in Rome when he wrote to the Philippians: "I have learned in whatever state I am, to be content: I know how to be abased, and I know how to abound . . . I can do all things through Christ who strengthens me" (Phil. 4:11–13). These verses are about contentment not *with* but *in* a negative situation.

Paul's contentment was not a mere feeling or a state of mind, however. It was an attitude that permeated his *behavior*. His ability to *display* contentment in his spirit to others was a powerful witness to his unsaved guards. Consider the results of Paul's willful choosing to be content within negative circumstances:

> I want you to know, brethren, that the things which happened to me have actually turned out for the furtherance of the gospel, so that it has become evident to the whole palace guard, and to all the rest, that my chains are in Christ; and most of the brethren in the Lord, having become confident by my chains, are much more bold to speak the word without fear . . . Christ is preached; and in this I rejoice, yes, and will rejoice. (Phil. 1:12–14, 18)

• *What new insights do you have into these verses from Philippians 1 and 4?*

_____

_____

• *In your life, have you struggled with experiencing true contentment?*

_____

_____

The Nature of Contentment

There are two main things that contentment is *not*:

1. *Contentment is not denial.* Paul was never in denial about his circumstances. He knew that he was imprisoned by Rome. He never tried to hide that fact or diminish the fact that he experienced needs. Paul wrote to the Philippians, "Everywhere and in all things I have learned both to be full and to be hungry,

both to abound and to suffer need" (Phil. 4:12). Paul knew the full spectrum of life—the very best of times and situations, and the very worst of times and situations.

Read what Paul wrote to Timothy. These are hardly the words of a man who is living in denial of the current gravity of his situation:

> At my first defense no one stood with me, but all for-sook me. May it not be charged against them. But the Lord stood with me and strengthened me, so that the message might be preached fully through me, and that all the Gentiles might hear. Also I was delivered out of the mouth of the lion. And the Lord will deliver me from every evil work and preserve me for His heavenly kingdom. To Him be glory forever and ever. Amen! (2 Tim. 4:16–18)

• *What new insights do you have into Philippians 4:12 and 2 Timothy 4:16–18?*

_____

_____

• *In your life or in the life of someone you know, has content-ment been confused with denial? Have you ever found yourself saying "Everything is just fine" when you knew deep within that everything was not fine? What were the results of your living in denial?*

_____

_____

2. *Contentment is not approval of external conditions.* To *accept* one's external conditions as a current state of fact is not the same as *approval* of those conditions. Did Paul want to be free? Absolutely! Did Paul believe that he had been unjustly impris-oned? Did he defend himself vigorously? Did he seek freedom through just and legal means? Most definitely he did!

To be content in a situation is not to say that the condition is good, or even acceptable. It is to say that the state of one's *soul* within that situation is good and acceptable. It is to say, "My external situation may be negative; I will work diligently to change it. But my internal situation is very positive; I will be steadfast in my relationship with the Lord."

Contentment is not a "settling down for a settled life" attitude. It is not throwing up one's hands and saying, "I give up." It is not throwing in the towel and refusing to work for positive changes. Contentment is not giving in to difficult situations or allowing a negative circumstance to dictate our response to life.

What Is Contentment?

Contentment is:

- dwelling peaceably in a current situation until that situation changes. We are to pray, believe, and look for change, but true contentment is trusting God to reveal both His methods and His timing for change.
- refusing to fall into the traps of greed, covetousness, or envy. We are to be content with the possessions we currently have, without coveting our neighbor's possessions, being envious of another's position, or seeking to hoard or consume far more than we truly can use or need.
- a pervasive attitude of "rest" that our relationship is right with the Lord. It is an attitude of confidence that God is working all things together for the perfection of His purposes. It is a perspective, a frame of mind, far more than it is a feeling.

- *Think back to a time when you truly experienced inner contentment. On what was your contentment based?*

_____

_____

What the Word Says	What the Word Says to Me
Then Moses was content to live with the man [Reuel, priest of	....

Midian], and he gave Zipporah his daughter to Moses. And she bore him a son. He called his name Gershom, for he said, "I have been a stranger in a foreign land."(Ex. 2:21–22)

Godliness with contentment is great gain. For we brought nothing into this world, and it is certain we can carry nothing out. And having food and clothing, with these we shall be content. (1 Tim. 6:6–8)

Let your conduct be without covetousness; be content with such things as you have. (Heb. 13:5)

Where envy and self-seeking exist, confusion and every evil thing are there. But the wisdom that is from above is first pure, then peaceable, gentle, willing to yield, full of mercy and good fruits, without partiality and without hypocrisy. Now the fruit of righteousness is sown in peace by those who make peace. (James 3:16–18)

How Can We Develop Inner Contentment?

The Bible gives us three things that we can do to develop inner contentment so that we truly live as "victors," even in situations in which we seem to be "losing the battle."

1. *Focus on the positive circumstances around you.* No situation or circumstance is 100 percent negative. There is always a positive side to every experience, every situation. Look for it. There *are* some good things around you even in the worst of times.

Refuse to wallow in a pity party. Refuse to complain, criticize, or justify a negative situation. Constant conversation or comments about a negative situation only make that situation loom larger in your own mind, as well as in the thinking of others around you.

Again, this focus on the positive is not a denial that negatives exist. Rather, it is a choice to put one's focus and attention on the positive things that can be built up, improved, encouraged, or praised.

When we focus on the positive, even as we recognize and work to change the negative, we live in "victory" over the enemy. We are in a much better position to bring about true change that results in positive growth and lasting reconciliation.

What the Word Says

Do all things without complaining and disputing, that you may become blameless and harmless, children of God without fault in the midst of a crooked and perverse generation, among whom you shine as lights in the world, holding fast the word of life. (Phil. 2:14–16)

Rejoice in the Lord. (Phil. 3:1)

Whatever things are true, whatever things are noble, whatever things are just, whatever things are pure, whatever things are lovely, whatever things are of

What the Word Says to Me

----

good report, if there is any
virtue and if there is anything
praiseworthy—meditate on
these things. (Phil. 4:8)

If your enemy is hungry,
give him bread to eat;
And if he is thirsty, give
him water to drink;
For so you will heap coals
of fire on his head,
And the LORD will reward you.
(Prov. 25:21–22)

2. *Witness to someone about the love of God and the saving grace of Jesus Christ.* Some people think that if they are going through a negative experience, others will not view them as being victorious spiritually and, therefore, will not receive a positive witness about Christ. Some fear that others will equate a negative circumstance with a lack of faith or punishment from God. The real problem is that people who are going through hard times often think these things about themselves!

No matter what you are experiencing—and no matter how grave the situation, how dire the circumstance, or how much pain is involved—you can *always* give a positive witness about Christ's sustaining grace, His forgiveness, His mercy, His love, and His authority over all evil. In pointing to Christ, you point to the source of every solution to every problem—not only your problem.

Choose to be a positive witness to Christ's saving, healing, delivering, and restoring power.

What the Word Says

What the Word Says to Me

Be watchful in all things,
endure afflictions, do the work

of an evangelist, fulfill your
ministry. (2 Tim. 4:5)

I charge you therefore before
God and the Lord Jesus Christ,
who will judge the living and the
dead at His appearing and His
kingdom: Preach the word! Be
ready in season and out of
season. (2 Tim. 4:1–2)

Do not be ashamed of the
testimony of our Lord, nor of
me His prisoner . . . Hold fast
the pattern of sound words
which you have heard from me,
in faith and love which are in
Christ Jesus . . . You therefore,
my son, be strong in the grace
that is in Christ Jesus. And the
things that you have heard from
me among many witnesses,
commit these to faithful men
who will be able to teach others
also. (2 Tim. 1:8, 13; 2:1–2)

• *In your life, have you found it difficult to speak to others
about Jesus when you experience a difficult time? In what
ways are you feeling challenged in your spirit?*

3. *Choose to act in a positive manner, seeking positive results.*
Don't act out of your pain, but out of your faith that God can
do something *good* in the midst of dark or troubling times.
When Paul found himself in prison in Rome, he founded a

church! He closed his letter to the Philippians this way: "The brethren who are with me greet you. All the saints greet you, but especially those who are of Caesar's household" (Phil. 4:21–22).

Members of the praetorian guard of Caesar—some of the ten thousand choice men who were the emperor's personal guards—were being won to Christ through Paul's imprisonment. Paul was not only evangelizing the men who were guarding him, but he also was teaching and strengthening these new converts, helping to establish a new branch to the church in Rome.

What good things might you do in the midst of a negative circumstance? What good works might you begin or continue? What good words might you speak?

Refuse to make decisions or take actions that will only make matters worse. Watch closely what you say to others, especially those who have hurt you or who you believe are responsible for your negative situation. Those who find themselves in a negative marital situation very often begin to speak almost immediately about separation or divorce. They often hurl very abusive and critical comments at the spouse with whom they are angry. Very often those who find themselves feeling guilty or hurt begin to lash out with accusations or threats. Actions such as these only intensify a negative situation—they do very little to bring healing and reconciliation.

> • *In your life, cite an incident in which you only made a bad situation worse by what you said or did. Can you also cite an incident in which you made a bad situation BETTER by what you said or did?*

_____

_____

What the Word Says

A soft answer turns away wrath,
But a harsh word stirs up anger.
The tongue of the wise uses

What the Word Says to Me

....

....

....

knowledge rightly, But the
mouth of fools pours forth fool-
ishness. (Prov. 15:1–2)

[Jesus taught,] "But I say to you
who hear: Love your enemies,
do good to those who hate you,
bless those who curse you, and
pray for those who spitefully use
you. To him who strikes you on
the one cheek, offer the other
also. And from him who takes
away your cloak, do not with-
hold your tunic either. Give to
everyone who asks of you. And
from him who takes away your
goods do not ask them back.
And just as you want men to do
to you, you also do to them
likewise." (Luke 6:27–31)

My beloved brethren, be
steadfast, immovable, always
abounding in the work of the
Lord, knowing that your labor
is not in vain in the Lord.
(1 Cor. 15:58)

Living as a "Victor"

Stop to think a moment about a person who exhibits these
traits:

- deep inner contentment based upon a right relationship with God;

- realistic about life, but working to change those things that are negative;
- focused on the positive;
- quick to give a word of witness about Jesus Christ; and
- engages in positive behaviors toward others, seeking positive results.

You would probably describe such a person as being victorious in their Christian walk!

That is precisely right. We are called to live victoriously because we are in association with the Victor of all life, Jesus Christ. Others who see us in the midst of trouble and trials should find their attention drawn toward and focused on Christ in us, rather than the problems that surround us. We should proclaim with our lives as well as our words, "Thanks be to God, who gives us the victory through our Lord Jesus Christ" (1 Cor. 15:57).

•*What new insights do you have into ways you can live victoriously even in the midst of trial and trouble?*

_____

_____

• *In what ways are you feeling challenged in your spirit?*

_____

_____

EIGHT

CONFRONTING FOUR GIANT FEARS

"Fear not!"

It is one of the foremost commands in the Bible. The Lord makes it very clear in His Word that He desires for His people to live in intimate relationship with Him forever—a relationship without fear of punishment—and in this world, to live *as overcomers of fear*. The Lord never chides people for feeling fear—it is a normal human response to pain, hurt, trouble, and trauma. But the Lord does call us to overcome fear with our faith.

We discussed fear briefly in an earlier lesson, but in this lesson I want to focus on the four great fears that all people face to some degree during their lifetimes. These fears can loom to giant-size proportions in times of trial or crisis.

The Bible addresses each of these four fears in a direct way and with many verses. We will only be able to deal with a few of the many references. If you struggle with fear in one of these areas, I encourage you to use a concordance and make a personal study of the *whole* of God's Word on the subject, including God's promises to help you overcome fear.

1. The Fear of Death

Psychologists tell us that the number one fear of all people is the fear of death. This certainly is understandable since death brings a degree of both finality and judgment with it. Once we die, we can no longer relive those moments that we wish we could have lived a different way. Things that we have done, or left undone, will be our legacy and reputation in the generations ahead. (See Jesus' parable in Luke 16:19–31.)

The Bible speaks of death as an appointment we all face: "It is appointed for men to die once" (Heb. 9:27). The Bible also speaks of judgment in relationship to death. This same verse in Hebrews continues, "It is appointed for men to die once, but after this the judgment." The Bible also holds out hope for the believer regarding judgment. Hebrews 9:28 concludes, "So Christ was offered once to bear the sins of many. To those who eagerly wait for Him He will appear a second time, apart from sin, for salvation."

• *What new insights do you have into Hebrews 9:27–28?*

_____

_____

Those who die in Christ are instantly with the Lord. They will see Him, be with Him, and live in a paradise that is free from sin. As Jesus said to the thief on the cross who believed in Him: "Assuredly, I say to you, today you will be with Me in Paradise" (Luke 23:43). As believers in Christ, we are not only saved from the consequences of our sin and promised eternal life, but we are going to be saved from this sinful world—we are going to live in an eternal home that is totally sin-free.

Paul described death as a "change"—one moment here, the next changed and with Christ forever. We will be free from our earthly bodies, which are prone to sickness, decay, and corruption. We will live in an incorruptible body described as being glorious, powerful, and immortal.

What a wonderful life lies just beyond death for the believer!

In times of trouble and trauma, hold on to that hope. Cling to it. Put your trust in the Lord to be the first One you see as you enter into eternity.

What the Word Says	What the Word Says to Me
The body is sown in corruption, it is raised in incorruption. It is sown in dishonor, it is raised in glory. It is sown in weakness, it is raised in power. It is sown a natural body, it is raised a spiritual body. (1 Cor. 15:42–44)	
As was the man of dust, so also are those who are made of dust; and as is the heavenly Man, so also are those who are heavenly. And as we have borne the image of the man of dust, we shall also bear the image of the heavenly Man. (1 Cor. 15:48–49)	
We shall be changed. For this corruptible must put on incorruption, and this mortal must put on immortality. So when this corruptible has put on incorruption, and this mortal has put on immortality, then shall be brought to pass the saying that is written: "Death is swallowed up in victory." "O Death, where is your sting? O Hades, where is your victory?" (1 Cor. 15:52–55)	

We are always confident, knowing that while we are at home in
the body we are absent from the
Lord . . . We are confident, yes,
well pleased rather to be absent
from the body and to be present
with the Lord. Therefore we
make it our aim, whether present
or absent, to be well pleasing to
Him. (2 Cor. 5:6, 8–9)

• *In your life, have you struggled with a fear of death? In what ways are you feeling challenged or comforted in your spirit?*

_____

_____

2. The Fear of Failure and Rejection

A major fear that people experience in times of trouble is a fear of failure. Sickness, divorce, loss of a job, an accident—all of these can be reasons for a person to feel as if he or she has "failed" in some way.

Why do we fear failure? The main reason seems to be that we believe our failure will cause others to reject us, distance themselves from us, or view us with disdain. We all want to be liked and to be in warm association with other people. We want to be appreciated, applauded, valued, and considered worthy. When we fail, we fear the loss of friendships, work relationships, family associations, and even loss of relationships with people who may be in the church.

The only failure that truly matters to the Lord, however, is a failure to accept Jesus Christ as one's Savior. That is the only "failure" on our part that has lasting consequences with our loving heavenly Father. All other failures we may experience are regarded by our Father as potential learning experiences for us, an opportunity to mold our character into greater conformity to Christ, and an opportunity for His own strength and power to be manifested.

The apostle Paul experienced a "thorn in the flesh" that seemed to be perceived by Paul and others as a sign of weakness or failure. Paul wrote, "Concerning this thing I pleaded with the Lord three times that it might depart from me. And He said to me, 'My grace is sufficient for you, for My strength is made perfect in weakness.'" Paul concluded about this failure—this lack of answered prayer, this ongoing weakness, "Therefore most gladly I will rather boast in my infirmities, that the power of Christ may rest upon me. Therefore I take pleasure in infirmities, in reproaches, in needs, in persecutions, in distresses, for Christ's sake. For when I am weak, then I am strong" (2 Cor. 12:7–10).

•*What new insights do you have into this passage from 2 Corinthians?*

_____

_____

We can also know with certainty from God's Word that no failure on our part will cause the Lord to leave us. Moses said to Joshua in the sight of all the Israelites: "Be strong and of good courage, for you must go with this people to the land which the LORD has sworn to their fathers to give them, and you shall cause them to inherit it. And the LORD, He is the One who goes before you. He will be with you, He will not leave you nor forsake you; do not fear nor be dismayed" (Deut. 31:7–8). This statement is echoed in Hebrews 13:5: "He Himself has said, 'I will never leave you nor forsake you.'"

• *How do you feel as you read these words of the Lord, "I will never leave you nor forsake you"?*

_____

_____

Nothing we do can cause the Lord to turn His back on us or disown His association with us. He is forever present with us, now and every moment of our future, on into eternity.

When we fail, the Lord requires only that we turn to Him and ask His forgiveness, His wisdom, and His help. We must be quick to obey the Lord if He shows us areas in which we must seek the forgiveness of others or make amends for our errors. Our humility before the Lord brings us to a place where He can heal us and restore us, and once again, bring us into close fellowship with other believers.

This does not mean that all broken relationships will be reconciled on this earth. The will and humility of *both* persons in a broken relationship must be involved for a relationship truly to be reconciled by God. It *does* mean that the Lord desires to heal all broken hearts.

• *In your life, have you experienced a failure that was followed by healing from the Lord?*

_____

_____

What the Word Says

The helpless commits himself to You;
You are the helper of the fatherless. (Ps. 10:14)

A father of the fatherless,
a defender of widows,
Is God in His holy habitation.
God sets the solitary in families;
He brings out those who are bound into prosperity. (Ps. 68:5–6)

[Jesus said,] "Lo, I am with you always, even to the end of the age." (Matt. 28:20)

What the Word Says to Me

_____

_____

_____

_____

_____

_____

_____

_____

_____

_____

_____

_____

For thus says the High
and Lofty One Who inhabits
eternity, whose name is Holy:
"I dwell in the high
and holy place,
With him who has a contrite
and humble spirit,
To revive the spirit of the humble,
And to revive the heart of the
contrite ones . . .I have seen his
ways, and will heal him;
I will also lead him,
And restore comforts to him
And to his mourners.
(Isa. 57:15, 18)

• *In your life, have you struggled with a fear of failure and rejection? In what ways are you feeling challenged in your spirit?*

---

3. The Fear of Material Loss

Times of tragedy, and especially tragedies that involve natural or economic disasters, often are accompanied by a great fear of material loss. We fear that we will lose our possessions that have given us a degree of comfort, status, and security. For some, the loss may be severe to the point of fearing homelessness, bankruptcy, or poverty.

One thing we need to remember always is that *all* things that we count as possessions have been given to us by the Lord. He is the One who gives us the ability to work, to create, to produce, and to acquire wealth. He is the One who presents opportunities to us and allows our efforts to prosper. As Ecclesiastes

5:19 tells us, "As for every man to whom God has given riches and wealth, and given him power to eat of it, to receive his heritage and rejoice in his labor—this is the gift of God."

The Lord asks us to trust *Him* to provide what we need, and admonishes us against putting our trust in possessions or money.

Furthermore, whatever we may *lose* in terms of material possessions, the Lord is able to *restore*. In times of loss, we must trust God to teach us the lessons He desires for us to learn and to restore to us anything that the enemy of our souls has stolen from us or destroyed.

What the Word Says

[Jesus taught,] "Therefore I say to you, do not worry about your life, what you will eat or what you will drink; nor about your body, what you will put on. Is not life more than food and the body more than clothing? Look at the birds of the air, for they neither sow nor reap nor gather into barns; yet your heavenly Father feeds them. Are you not of more value than they? . . . Consider the lilies of the field, how they grow: they neither toil nor spin; and yet I say to you that even Solomon in all his glory was not arrayed like one of these. Now if God so clothes the grass of the field, which today is, and tomorrow is thrown into the oven, will He not much more clothe you, O you of little faith?" (Matt. 6:25–26, 28–30)

What the Word Says to Me

[Jesus said,] "The thief does not come except to steal, and to kill, and to destroy. I have come that they may have life, and that they may have it more abundantly."
(John 10:10)

Be glad then,
you children of Zion,
And rejoice in the
LORD your God;
For He has given you the
former rain faithfully,
And He will cause the rain
to come down for you—
The former rain,
And the latter rain
in the first month.
The threshing floors shall
be full of wheat,
And the vats shall overflow
with new wine and oil.
So I will restore to you the
years that the swarming
locust has eaten . . .
You shall eat in plenty
and be satisfied,
And praise the name
of the LORD your God,
Who has dealt
wondrously with you;
And My people shall
never be put to shame.
(Joel 2:23–26)

• In your life, have you struggled with a fear of material loss? In what ways are you feeling challenged in your spirit?

_____

_____

4. The Fear of Change

In times of trauma and hardship, many people feel as if their entire world is "shaken" and that "nothing will ever be the same again." They fear the unknowns of the future. They do not trust God to deal kindly with them in the days ahead. In their thinking, all change is "bad change."

The fact is, a great deal of change is for our *good*!

Jeremiah was a prophet who spoke the words of the Lord to Israel in a time of great upheaval and turmoil in the nation. The people longed to hear words of comfort from the prophet—they deeply desired a message that would say the Lord was going to deliver them from being taken captive by Babylon. The Lord, however, told them that they would be taken captive for seventy years!

But the word of the Lord to His people did not end with that message. The Lord also told His people, "The days are coming . . . that I will bring back from captivity My people Israel and Judah . . . And I will cause them to return to the land that I gave to their fathers, and they shall possess it" (Jer. 30:3). Furthermore, the Lord said,

Do not fear, O My servant Jacob . . .
Nor be dismayed, O Israel;
For behold, I will save you from afar,
And your seed from the land of their captivity.
Jacob shall return, have rest and be quiet,
And no one shall make him afraid.
For I am with you . . . to save you;
Though I make a full end of all nations where I have scattered you,
Yet I will not make a complete end of you. (Jer. 30:10–11)

The Lord used the years of captivity to teach very important lessons to His people—lessons that prepared them for the return of their land and future prosperity.

Furthermore, the Lord said to His people: "I know the thoughts that I think toward you . . . thoughts of peace and not of evil, to give you a future and a hope" (Jer. 29:11).

> • *What new insights do you have into these passages from Jeremiah?*

_____

_____

Any time we are facing change, we must remember that the Lord has the same desire for us that He had for the Israelites—His plans for us are ones that lead to peace and not evil. He has a good future for us, and, therefore, we must have hope!

Choose to see change as a process of good that the Lord is unfolding in your life. Trust Him to lead you to greater prosperity and wholeness.

What the Word Says	What the Word Says to Me
[The Lord said through Jeremiah,] "I have loved you with an everlasting love; Therefore with lovingkindness I have drawn you. Again I will build you, and you shall be rebuilt." (Jer. 31:3–4)	_____ _____ _____ _____ _____ _____ _____
The LORD is my shepherd; I shall not want. He makes me to lie down in green pastures; He leads me beside the still waters.	_____ _____ _____ _____

He restores my soul;
He leads me in the paths of
righteousness
For His name's sake.
Yea, though I walk through the
valley of the shadow of death,
I will fear no evil;
For You are with me;
Your rod and Your staff,
they comfort me.
You prepare a table before me in
the presence of my enemies;
You anoint my head with oil;
My cup runs over.
Surely goodness and mercy
shall follow me
All the days of my life;
And I will dwell in the
house of the LORD
Forever. (Ps. 23:1–6)

For the Lamb who is in the
midst of the throne will shep-
herd them and lead them to
living fountains of waters. And
God will wipe away every tear
from their eyes. (Rev. 7:17)

• *In your life, have you struggled with a fear of change? In what ways are you feeling challenged in your spirit?*

Saying "No" to Fear

Faith is saying "no" to fear and "yes" to God.
Our faith that we will be with the Lord beyond our death

gives us the courage to say no to a fear of death.

Our faith that God will never forsake us, regardless of how we may fail, gives us the courage to say no to a fear of failure and rejection.

Our faith that God desires to prosper us and meet our needs gives us the courage to say no to a fear of material loss.

Our faith that God is leading us through life, step-by-step, gives us the courage to say no to a fear of change.

Our faith is rooted in who God is and what God will do. Choose to be a person who walks by faith and who responds to life with faith, rather than be a person who cowers before trouble in fear.

Let us remember always the words of Paul to the Corinthians: "We walk by faith, not by sight" (2 Cor. 5:7). Choose to believe for what God *will* do on your behalf, rather than be paralyzed by what you see happening around you.

> • *What new insights do you have into ways you can overcome the fear associated with times of trouble?*

_____

_____

NINE

A FOCUS ON OUR DESTINY AS BELIEVERS

What is your destiny as a believer?

Certainly all of us as followers of Christ have the destiny of an eternal life with our loving heavenly Father in heaven. That is our ultimate destiny.

But what is your destiny here on earth? What is it that God purposes for you, and for every other believer?

To a degree, our purpose on this earth is highly personalized. We are unique creatures, gifted and talented in unique ways, and called to unique ministries within a unique sphere of influence. We each face the challenge of discovering *precisely* what it is that the Lord created us to be and to do.

In a more general way, however, all of us are given a purpose as *followers of Christ*. In this lesson, we are going to focus on five of these general purposes related to our destiny as believers.

1. Our Destiny Is to Show God's Love to the World

Part of our purpose as believers is to express God's love to a love-starved world.

Every Christian should both believe and display his belief to others that God loves him. God's love is infinite and unconditional. It is far greater, far richer, and far more meaningful than any of us can fully grasp or accept. Nevertheless, we are to *grow* in our ability to accept God's love and in our ability to express God's love to others. That is part of our destiny and purpose on this earth.

God's love does not change. God's love does not waver, wax, or wane. It is constant. As James says, "There is no variation or shadow of turning" with God's love (see James 1:17). Love is part of His unchanging nature (1 John 4:8).

God's love is unconditional. God loves you and me as much as He will ever love us, even though we are each far from perfect. Romans 5:8 tells us plainly, "God demonstrates His own love toward us, in that while we were still sinners, Christ died for us." Nothing you can do, or anyone else can ever do to you, can separate you from God's love. And, nothing you do can ever cause God to love you more. He already loves you with an infinite love.

God's love motivates Him toward our blessing and perfection. God loves us *as* we are, but because He loves us, He does not *leave us as we are.* God's desire is that we draw closer and closer to Him. As He conforms us more and more into the character-likeness of Jesus Christ, we become more and more whole, and we grow into greater and greater intimacy and fellowship with Him.

Our response to God's love. Our response to God's love is very clear: We are commanded to love others. Our purpose and destiny on this earth are to receive God's love and then display God's love to others.

Especially in troubled times, the world needs to experience God's love. It is in the darkest hours that love shines the brightest.

> • *In your life, have you experienced the love of God flowing to you from other people during a dark or difficult time of trouble? How did you feel? What did that mean to you?*

_____

_____

What the Word Says	What the Word Says to Me
[Jesus taught,] "'You shall love the LORD your God with all your heart, with all your soul, and with all your mind.' This is the first and great commandment. And the second is like it: 'You shall love your neighbor as yourself.' On these two commandments hang all the Law and the Prophets." (Matt. 22:37–40)	
If we love one another, God abides in us, and His love has been perfected in us. (1 John 4:12)	
We love Him because He first loved us. If someone says, "I love God," and hates his brother, he is a liar; for he who does not love his brother whom he has seen, how can he love God whom he has not seen? And this commandment we have from Him: that he who loves God must love his brother also. (1 John 4:19–21)	

2. Our Destiny Is to Proclaim Jesus As the Savior

Part of your purpose on this earth is to receive Jesus Christ as your Savior, and then to proclaim Him as the Savior to others through your words and your deeds. What is our message of salvation to be? Paul stated it well in writing to the Colossians:

> He [God] has delivered us from the power of darkness and conveyed us into the kingdom of the Son of His love, in whom we have redemption through His blood, the forgiveness of sins . . . For it pleased the Father that in Him all the fullness should dwell, and by Him to reconcile all things to Himself, by Him, whether things on earth or things in heaven, having made peace through the blood of His cross. And you, who once were alienated and enemies in your mind by wicked works, yet now He has reconciled in the body of His flesh through death, to present you holy, and blameless, and above reproach in His sight. (Col. 1:13–14, 19–22)

We are to proclaim to others that

- they do not need to live with a sin nature, steeped in guilt and shame before God.
- Jesus Christ died as God's atoning sacrifice for sin so that they do not need to reap the consequences of their sin, which is eternal separation from God.
- we can experience salvation through believing in Jesus Christ as God's atoning sacrifice and accepting what He did on the cross as being on our behalf.
- when we receive Jesus Christ as our Savior, Christ sends the Holy Spirit to indwell us so that we might live a life that is blameless and holy before God.

- *What additional insights do you have into this passage from Colossians?*

_____

_____

Jesus Christ did not only come to save us from *sin*, but to save us from *evil's hold on our lives*. We can live in freedom from the bondage of a nature that desires to sin. We can live *as unto the Lord*.

What good news this is! We are to be ambassadors—witnesses, messengers—of this good news to all we encounter. When times are unsettled or difficult, the world is far more ready to hear this message of Jesus Christ as Savior. We must be quick to speak of the saving love of God, manifested through Jesus' death on the cross, to others who are experiencing trouble or who may be facing death.

What the Word Says	What the Word Says to Me
We have seen and testify that the Father has sent the Son as Savior of the world. Whoever confesses that Jesus is the Son of God, God abides in him, and he in God. (1 John 4:14–15)	
We are ambassadors for Christ, as though God were pleading through us: we implore you on Christ's behalf, be reconciled to God. For He made Him who knew no sin to be sin for us, that we might become the righteousness of God in Him. (2 Cor. 5:20–21)	

• *How do you feel about your purpose on this earth as being an ambassador of Jesus Christ, the Savior? In what ways are you feeling challenged in your spirit?*

_____

_____

3. Our Destiny Is to Live a Godly Life

Our destiny as believers is to live a godly life and to keep God's commandments to the very best of our ability. Our purpose is to show others, through our behavior and our conversations, that it *is* possible to live a pure, victorious, peaceful, joyful life on this earth. Our purpose is to reflect a life that is totally reliant upon the Holy Spirit for guidance into right decisions, right choices, and right actions.

When times of trouble arise, those in the world look for examples of goodness. They look for those who are living in purity and who have faith and confidence. They look for examples that say to them, "Yes, it is possible even in the midst of terrible circumstances, to serve God." You are called by God to be such an example. Your destiny and purpose on this earth are to live a righteous life according to all the Lord commands you.

What the Word Says	What the Word Says to Me
When you were slaves of sin . . . What fruit did you have then in the things of which you are now ashamed? For the end of those things is death. But now having been set free from sin, and having become slaves of God, you have your fruit to holiness, and the end, everlasting life. (Rom 6:20–22)	....
You are the temple of the living God. As God has said: "I will dwell in them And walk among them. I will be their God, And they shall be My people."	....

Therefore
"Come out from among them
And be separate,
says the Lord.
Do not touch what is unclean,
And I will receive you."
"I will be a Father to you,
And you shall be my sons
and daughters,
Says the LORD Almighty."
Therefore, having these
promises, beloved, let us cleanse
ourselves from all filthiness of
the flesh and spirit, perfecting
holiness in the fear of God.
(2 Cor. 6:16–7:1)

The fruit of the Spirit is love,
joy, peace, longsuffering, kindness, goodness, faithfulness,
gentleness, self-control.
Against such there is no law.
And those who are Christ's
have crucified the flesh with its
passions and desires. If we live
in the Spirit, let us also walk in
the Spirit. (Gal. 5:22–25)

His divine power has given to
us all things that pertain to life
and godliness . . . that through
these you may be partakers of
the divine nature, having
escaped the corruption that is
in the world through lust. But
also for this very reason, giving

all diligence, add to your faith
virtue, to virtue knowledge, to
knowledge self-control, to self-
control perseverance, to
perseverance godliness, to godliness brotherly kindness, and
to brotherly kindness love. For
if these things are yours and
abound, you will be neither
barren nor unfruitful in the
knowledge of our Lord Jesus
Christ. (2 Peter 1:3–8)

4. Our Destiny Is to Serve Others

We each have been given both natural gifts and ministry gifts
in order that we might *serve* others. Part of our purpose on this
earth is to be involved in active ministry to others—which
means the "meeting of needs" in their lives. To the best of our
ability, we are to meet the practical and material needs of those
who have material needs. We are to minister to the emotional,
physical, and spiritual needs of others who have needs in these
areas. We are to pray for others, serve others, help others, give
to others, and be present for others.

Times of trouble and trauma are times of great need. Our
purpose on this earth is to meet needs in the name of Jesus.

> • *Recall several instances or ways in which you have received
> the ministry help of others in times of need.*

What the Word Says

Now Peter and John went up
together to the temple at the
hour of prayer, the ninth hour.

What the Word Says to Me

And a certain man lame from his mother's womb was carried, whom they laid daily at the gate of the temple which is called Beautiful, to ask alms from those who entered the temple; who, seeing Peter and John about to go into the temple, asked for alms. And fixing his eyes on him, with John, Peter said, "Look at us." So he gave them his attention, expecting to receive something from them. Then Peter said, "Silver and gold I do not have, but what I do have I give you: In the name of Jesus Christ of Nazareth, rise up and walk." And he took him by the right hand and lifted him up, and immediately his feet and ankle bones received strength. So he, leaping up, stood and walked and entered the temple with them—walking, leaping, and praising God. (Acts 3:1–8)

For as we have many members in one body, but all the members do not have the same function, so we, being many, are one body in Christ, and individually members of one another. Having then gifts differing according to the grace that is given to us, let us use them. (Rom. 12:4–6)

Be kindly affectionate to one
another with brotherly love, in
honor giving preference to one
another; not lagging in diligence,
fervent in spirit, serving the
Lord; rejoicing in hope, patient
in tribulation, continuing stead-
fastly in prayer; distributing to
the needs of the saints, given to
hospitality. (Rom. 12:10–13)

5. Our Destiny Is to Praise God in All Situations

Part of our destiny and purpose on this earth is to praise
God. Jesus said that if we don't praise God, the stones will cry
out in praise (see Luke 19:37–40 below). God delights in our
praise. He responds to our praise. He uses our praise to defeat
our enemies.

In times of struggle and difficulty, it is especially important
that we fulfill our destiny to praise God. The world watches
and listens. Will we curse God in times of trouble, as Job's wife
encouraged him to do, or will we praise God for who He is and
what we believe He will do on our behalf? May we always
choose to lift our voices in praise!

> • *How do you feel when others around you praise God and
> give voice to His majesty?*

What the Word Says

Then, as He [Jesus] was now
drawing near the descent of
the Mount of Olives, the whole

What the Word Says to Me

multitude of the disciples began
to rejoice and praise God with a
loud voice for all the mighty
works they had seen, saying:
'Blessed is the King who comes
in the name of the LORD!'
Peace in heaven and glory
in the highest!"
And some of the Pharisees
called to Him from the crowd,
"Teacher, rebuke Your disciples."
But He answered and said to
them, "I tell you that if these
should keep silent, the stones
would immediately cry out."
(Luke 19:37–40)

Praise the LORD!
Praise God in His sanctuary;
Praise Him in His mighty
firmament!
Praise Him for His
mighty acts;
Praise Him according
to His excellent greatness!
Praise Him with the sound
of the trumpet;
Praise Him
with the lute and harp!
Praise Him with the
timbrel and dance;
Praise Him with stringed
instruments and flutes!
Praise Him with loud cymbals;
Praise Him with clashing cymbals!

Let everything that has breath
praise the LORD.
Praise the LORD! (Ps. 150:1–6)

A Source of Encouragement

What type of person do you desire to have with you in a time of trouble? Isn't it a person who is loving toward you and who reminds you of God's love . . . a person who reminds you that Jesus Christ is your Savior and that you are forever secure in God's forgiveness . . . a person who lives by example a godly life . . . a person who is quick to see your needs and attempts to meet them . . . a person who voices praise to God? We are called by God to be just that type of person to others.

Our destiny and purpose on the earth are to *be* Christ-followers—to love others, serve others, praise God, and live godly lives!

What an important and special purpose that is, and especially so when the entire world seems to be turned upside-down.

•*What new insights do you have into the purpose God has for you in times of trouble and crisis?*

_____

_____

• *In what ways are you feeling challenged in your spirit?*

_____

_____

TEN

FIVE PRAYERS GOD ANSWERS IN ROUGH TIMES

How shall we pray in times of trouble?

Is it right to pray that God removes our trouble, heals our bodies, reconciles our marriages, or removes our pain? Absolutely!

The Bible encourages us to pray diligently in times of trouble, and to do so with faith, trusting God to act for our eternal benefit and according to His perfect methods and timing.

In this lesson, we will look at five prayers that we are wise to pray in times of trouble.

1. "Lord, Alleviate This Pressure"

In the Bible, stress and pressure are often described in terms of "oppression"—a feeling of heaviness, as if the weight of the world is on one's shoulders. Jesus said that He came to fulfill these words of the prophet Isaiah:

> The Spirit of the Lord God is upon Me,
> Because the LORD has anointed Me

To preach good tidings to the poor;
He has sent Me to heal the brokenhearted,
To proclaim liberty to the captives,
And the opening of the prison to those who are bound . . .
To comfort all who mourn,
To console those who mourn in Zion,
To give them beauty for ashes,
The oil of joy for mourning,
The garment of praise for the spirit of heaviness.
(Isa. 61:1–3)

When we are feeling oppressed, stressed out, under too much pressure, or frustrated because life seems overwhelming, we need to pray that the Lord will rebuke the enemy for our sake and restore our joy.

•*What new insights do you have into Isaiah 61:1-3?*

_____

_____

The Lord also desires that we live free of worry and anxiety. Worry, which is a form of doubt, can cause us to feel great pressure. The more we worry, the less we sleep, the more likely we are to make hurried and unwise decisions, and the more prone we are to accidents. Worry *increases* pressure, rather than releases it. If worry is the source of your pressure, ask the Lord to help you trust Him more (see Mark 9:24).

What the Word Says	What the Word Says to Me
God anointed Jesus of Nazareth with the Holy Spirit and with power, who went about doing good and healing all who were oppressed by the devil, for God was with Him. (Acts 10:38)	_____ _____ _____ _____ _____ _____ _____

Why do You hide Your face,
And forget our affliction and
our oppression?
For our soul is bowed down to
the dust . . .
Arise for our help,
And redeem us for Your
mercies' sake. (Ps. 44:24–26)

Jesus said to him, "If you can
believe, all things are possible
to him who believes." Immediately the father of the child
cried out and said with tears,
"Lord, I believe; help my
unbelief!" (Mark 9:23–24)

• *In what ways are you feeling challenged in your spirit?*

2. "Lord, Clarify This Confusion"

The Lord is never the instigator of confusion. His commandments are clear. His path is well lighted. His message is
direct. His desire is for order and peace among His people. As
Paul wrote to the Ephesians, "Walk worthy of the calling with
which you were called . . . endeavoring to keep the unity of the
Spirit in the bond of peace" (Eph. 4:1, 3). Paul also admonished the church, "How is it then, brethren? Whenever you
come together, each of you has a psalm, has a teaching, has a
tongue, has a revelation, has an interpretation. Let all things
be done for edification . . . Let all things be done decently and
in order" (1 Cor. 14:26, 40).

Two words are closely related to *confusion* in the Bible: *deceit* and *hypocrisy*. Deceit is a lie—and lies always breed confusion. Hypocrisy is being two-faced—and again, hypocrisy results in confusion. Any time we are confused, we should look to see if deceit or hypocrisy is the cause of our confusion.

The prayer we must pray when we feel confused is this: "Lord, shed the light of Your truth on this matter. Deliver me from hypocrisy! Bring order to my thinking. Bring order to this group [or this marriage, or this meeting, or this place, or this experience]."

What the Word Says

What the Word Says to Me

For God is not the author of confusion but of peace. (1 Cor. 14:33)

But the wisdom that is from above is first pure, then peaceable, gentle, willing to yield, full of mercy and good fruits, without partiality and without hypocrisy. Now the fruit of righteousness is sown in peace by those who make peace. (James 3:17–18)

Vindicate me, O God . . . Oh, deliver me from the deceitful and unjust man! (Ps. 43:1)

Jesus spoke to them again, saying, "I am the light of the world. He who follows Me shall not walk in darkness, but have the light of life." (John 8:12)

• *In what ways are you feeling challenged in your spirit?*

_____

_____

3. "Lord, Help Me with This Pain"

The pain that we experience in rough times is not only physical, but also emotional and spiritual. We *ache* in sorrow, grief, and as a result of mental anguish.

When you are experiencing pain, ask the Lord to heal you—both in your body and in your emotions!

What the Word Says	What the Word Says to Me
Is anyone among you suffering? Let him pray . . . Is anyone among you sick? Let him call for the elders of the church, and let them pray over him, anointing him with oil in the name of the Lord. And the prayer of faith will save the sick, and the Lord will raise him up. (James 5:13–15)	
Pray for one another, that you may be healed. (James 5:16)	
Redeem me from the oppression of man, That I may keep Your precepts. (Ps. 119:134)	
I am like a broken vessel. But as for me, I trust in You, O LORD; I say, "You are my God." (Ps. 31:12, 14)	

Have mercy on me, O LORD,

for I am weak;

O LORD, heal me, for my

bones are troubled.

My soul also is greatly troubled...

Return, O LORD, deliver me!

(Ps. 6:2–4)

• *In what ways are you feeling challenged in your spirit?*

4. "Lord, Help Me Withstand This Temptation"

We must never think that the Lord tempts us to do evil. James wrote very plainly about this: "Let no one say when he is tempted, 'I am tempted by God'; for God cannot be tempted by evil, nor does He Himself tempt anyone. But each one is tempted when he is drawn away by his own desires and enticed. Then, when desire has conceived, it gives birth to sin; and sin, when it is full-grown, brings forth death" (James 1:13–15).

The word for "tempt" in the Bible can also mean "test." The Lord does test us from time to time—not for *His* sake, but so that *we* will discover areas of weakness, error, or rebellion in our lives. The purpose of the Lord's tests is that we might make changes in our lives and move on to greater strength and to a deeper level of intimacy with the Lord. But—and this is very important—the Lord never tests us by tempting us to break His commandments. The devil is the one who is called the "tempter" in the Bible—he is the one who comes to entice us to do evil (see Matt. 4:4). When we feel a temptation to do evil, we must pray quickly as Jesus taught us, "Deliver us from the evil one" (Matt. 6:13).

Furthermore, the Lord never allows the enemy to tempt us beyond what we are able to bear. He always provides a way of escape for us (see 1 Cor. 10:13). We are wise to ask the Lord to reveal to us His escape plan!

What the Word Says	What the Word Says to Me
No temptation has overtaken you except such as is common to man; but God is faithful, who will not allow you to be tempted beyond what you are able, but with the temptation will also make the way of escape, that you may be able to bear it. (1 Cor. 10:13)	....
[Jesus taught us to pray,] "And do not lead us into temptation, But deliver us from the evil one." (Matt. 6:13)	....
Direct my steps by Your word, And let no iniquity have domin- ion over me. (Ps. 119:133)	....

• *In what ways are you feeling challenged in your spirit?*

_____

_____

5. "Lord, Give Me Strength to Endure"

The Lord makes numerous promises in His Word that He will be the "strong right arm" of those who love Him and obey His commandments. He tells us that He is our rock, our fortress, our high tower—all of which are places of refuge a person might run to when enduring rough times.

The Lord gives us His power so that we might outlast and overcome hard times, He gives us His presence and authority so that we might fight *and win* spiritual battles, and He gives us His Word so that we might defeat the enemy with it (see Matt. 4:1–11). He sends His holy angels to be ministering servants on our behalf and to defend us in our stand against evil.

When you are experiencing a rough time, pray to the Lord for enduring strength! Pray for spiritual power!

What the Word Says	What the Word Says to Me
But You, O Lord,	
are a God full of compassion,	
and gracious,	
Longsuffering and abundant	
in mercy and truth.	
Oh, turn to me, and have	
mercy on me!	
Give Your strength to Your	
servant,	
And save the son of Your	
maidservant. (Ps. 86:15–16)	
But You, O LORD,	
do not be far from Me;	
O My Strength, hasten to help	
me! (Ps. 22:19)	
My soul, wait silently	
for God alone,	
For my expectation is from Him.	
He only is my rock and my	
salvation;	
He is my defense;	
I shall not be moved.	
In God is my salvation	
and my glory;	
The rock of my strength,	
And my refuge, is in God.	
(Ps. 62:5–7)	

The LORD is my light and my
salvation;
Whom shall I fear?
The LORD is the strength
of my life;
Of whom shall I be afraid?
For in the time of trouble
He shall hide me in His pavilion;
In the secret place of His
tabernacle
He shall hide me;
He shall set me high upon
a rock. (Ps. 27:1, 5)

• *In what ways are you feeling challenged in your spirit?*

_____

_____

Expect God to Answer!

When you pray, expect God to both hear and answer your prayers. Trust Him to be faithful to His Word and to deliver you from the anguish of your difficult experience. Trust Him to give you peace in your heart that is beyond understanding.

Make Philippians 4:6–7 your hope as you pray: "In everything by prayer and supplication, with thanksgiving, let your requests be made known to God; and the peace of God, which surpasses all understanding, will guard your hearts and minds through Christ Jesus."

• *In your life, have you had experiences in praying the five prayers of this lesson? What were the results?*

_____

_____

• *In what ways is the Lord challenging you to pray right now?*

_____

_____

CONCLUSION

TAKE HEART AND HAVE COURAGE!

Of one thing you can be certain in any time of trouble, trauma, suffering, hardship, difficulty, pain, or tragedy: The Lord is with you! Time and again in His Word, the Lord assures us of His presence:

- "The LORD is with you while you are with Him. If you seek Him, He will be found by you" (2 Chron. 15:2).
- "Stand still and see the salvation of the LORD, who is with you...Do not fear or be dismayed" (2 Chron. 20:17).
- "Do not be afraid of him," says the LORD, "for I am with you, to save you and deliver you from his hand" (Jer. 42:11).
- "Be strong, all you people of the land," says the LORD, "and work; for I am with you" (Hag. 2:4).

Jesus also said to His disciples, "I am with you always" (Matt. 28:20).

Truly, if the Lord is with us, and "If God is for us, who can be against us?" (Rom. 8:31).

When rough times come, immerse yourself in God's Word. Read His promises to you, His beloved child. Read about His power, His strength, His wisdom, and His love. Read how He has helped countless men and women through the ages as they trusted in Him. Read about His saving, delivering, and restoring power.

The more you read and study God's Word, the stronger your faith will grow.

The more you trust God, the more you will grow in your understanding that He is trustworthy in all things, at all times.

The more you take courage in the Lord's presence with you, the more secure you will feel . . . even in the most troubling of times and the most trying of circumstances.

The Lord *is* our Security, every moment of our lives.

NOTES